S0-FCR-152

# THE ENGLISH WOMEN NOVELISTS AND THEIR CONNECTION WITH THE FEMINIST MOVEMENT

(1688-1797)

By

Joyce M. Horner

*FOLCROFT LIBRARY EDITIONS / 1973*

**Library of Congress Cataloging in Publication Data**

Horner, Joyce Mary, 1903-
The English women novelists and their connections with the feminist movement (1688-1797).

Reprint of the 1930 ed., which was issued as v. 11, no. 1-3, of Smith College studies in modern languages.
Bibliography: p.
1. Women as authors--Great Britain. 2. English fiction--18th century--History and criticism.
3. Woman--Social and moral questions. I. Title.
II. Series: Smith College studies in modern languages, v. 11, no. 1-3.
PR119.H6 1973 823'.03 73-1613
ISBN 0-8414-2059-9 (lib bdg)

Vol. XI, Nos. 1, 2, 3. Oct., 1929; Jan.; Apr., 1930

# Smith College Studies in Modern Languages

## THE ENGLISH WOMEN NOVELISTS AND THEIR CONNECTION WITH THE FEMINIST MOVEMENT

(1688-1797)

By

Joyce M. Horner

NORTHAMPTON, MASSACHUSETTS

# PREFACE

This study is reproduced, with very little alteration, from a thesis written in fulfilment of the requirements of the Master of Arts degree at Smith College. The title is perhaps misleading. The word "feminism" in its short life—there is no record of its usage before 1851—has changed a good deal in meaning. In the 1888 edition of the *New English Dictionary* it is among the words described as rare and is defined simply as "the qualities of females." Today it has acquired a more specific connotation. H. W. Fowler, in his *Modern English Usage,* defines it as "faith in women: advocacy of the rights of women," while the *New Standard Dictionary* goes a step further in defining it as "the doctrine of mental and social equality of women with men."

Feminism has become a movement and a "cause" and the word sounds in some ears like a war-cry; it is, therefore, possible that the words "feminist movement" on the title-page may give a false impression. It should be clearly understood that this is in no sense a history of the early days of the feminist movement. The women with whose history it is concerned would not have called themselves feminists, even had the word existed for them to use. The reader will hear in the following pages of women militant and triumphant, but it was their individual battles they were fighting, not the battles of their whole sex. Yet, as it is the unconscious workers for a cause who often serve it best, so these women who forced themselves upon the public notice, by writing novels at a time when few women could write even a decent letter, indirectly did great service to women in general. Without them it would have been useless for the later theorist to proclaim to the world the glory of women's rights. Those women who intruded into the world of men and proved their capacities are perhaps of more ultimate importance in the history of feminism than all those others who sat at home and "reasoned high" of the capacities women might show if they had the chance.

I have attempted, in the second part of this study, to come to some conclusions, however tentative, on the much-debated question of the feminine mind. My excuse for combining this with the historical outline contained in Part I is, that with any discussion on women's rights, some discussion of women's powers inevitably arises. Literature is always a favourite test case in debates on feminism and always the old challenge goes forth: "Why is there no woman Shakespeare?" It seemed to me, then, not unfitting, having followed the struggles of these early writers in their lives, to turn to their works and try to discover whether these show any characteristics which we may call specifically feminine. Their actual achievement, if anything, is going to show why women are not Shakespeares. At the same time it may reveal them as capable of some things of which men would not be capable. To find a "feminine" mind might seem the deathblow to the hopes of the ardent feminist who would like to prove the equation "feminine equals masculine." Yet if the female mind is different in kind from the male, surely there is comfort in the fact that women may make a contribution to literature, peculiar to themselves. All this, I maintain, is connected however loosely with what is implied by the words "feminist movement" and a connection is all that is claimed by the title of this study.

I should like here to thank Miss Mary Ellen Chase of Smith College, under whose guidance my thesis was written and without whose help and encouragement it never could have been written. I should like to thank also Miss Marjorie Hope Nicolson of Smith College for her many valuable suggestions and for her patience in endeavouring to bring down Philosophy to the level of one to whom years will never bring the philosophic mind. Lastly, I should like to express my indebtedness to Professor Gordon of the University of Oxford for, although he is quite unaware of it, it was a chance remark in a lecture of his that was responsible for starting me along the trail I have here explored.

January 1930.

CONTENTS

## INTRODUCTION

The purpose of this study is twofold. Its aim, in the first place, is to take a survey of the position of the woman author from the period of her early struggles, to the time when she had established her right to a place in the world of letters and was accepted without comment by the world in general. Its second aim is to investigate the works of a few of these women to determine whether they show any qualities peculiarly feminine. The first part will be concerned with facts, the plain facts of the existence of these women; the second part will deal in speculations to which the facts have given rise; the one deals with feminism in its modern meaning, "advocacy of the rights of women" and the other takes us back to the older sense of the word—"the qualities of females."

It is with novelists only that we are here concerned. But it is difficult to begin upon the life of Aphra Behn, the first English woman novelist, without saying something of the women who lived and wrote before her. There were learned ladies in England in Tudor times and even before[1]—we have only to turn over the pages of Ballard's *Memoirs of Learned Ladies in the Fifteenth and Sixteenth Centuries* to be impressed by their numbers and by their exalted station—but all these were scholars rather than writers. The name of Lady Jane Grey, "to whom all pleasures were but a shadoe to that pleasure which she found in Plato," carries with it a suggestion of the sweetness and light, the grace and comeliness of learning, but her pen has left us no enduring monument. Queen Elizabeth may have been learned in five languages and able to confound her ambassadors with floods of Latin, but little evidence remains of her "learned, delicate and noble Muse." Even the Countess of Pembroke's fame rests rather on the fact that she was "Sidney's sister, Pembroke's mother" than on her translations from the French and Italian, while that "choice lady" Anne Coke,[2] "eminent for piety, virtue and learning, being exquisitely skilled

[1] For an account of these ladies and their works see: Ballard *Memoirs of Learned Ladies in the Fifteenth and Sixteenth Centuries.* London, 1773; Reynolds, Myra *Learned Lady in England*, Boston, 1920.

[2] Rawley, *Life of Bacon*, 1657. (Bacon's *Works*, Spedding, Ellis and Heath. Vol. I, p. 3, New York, 1905.)

for a woman in the Greek and Latin tongues," is remembered now because she was the mother of Francis Bacon. It is with pleasure and respect that we contemplate this little group of royal and noble ladies who devoted themselves, not by compulsion, to the task of getting wisdom and getting understanding. They were not without their influence on the life of the court and on the work of courtier poets like Raleigh and Spenser, but they never attained to more than a passive equality with the men. They themselves are greater than their works, even after the passing of three centuries.

A long period without bud or blossom followed this early flowering-time of women's genius. Some few in the retirement of country houses still found leisure amid the "hoarse encumbrances of household care" to learn their Greek and Latin grammar, to compose their prayers and hymns and to record in notebooks the struggles of their souls, but on the whole it is only rarely that a woman's voice is heard during the first half of the seventeenth century. Either because of the changed tone of court life, or because of the Civil War, which broke in rudely upon the poet's meditations, we find women relapsing almost into silence. But with the Restoration came a change, and a change that was more than a mere return to the state of affairs at the court of Elizabeth. For, from this time onward, we find women writing not only as amateurs in a small literary circle, not only as devotees in the privacy of their homes, but as authors practising their craft in the public eye and later *for* the public eye.

Among the predecessors of Aphra Behn two women in particular deserve notice—Katharine Phillips (the Matchless Orinda) and Margaret, Duchess of Newcastle, each of whom won for herself the title of "glory of her sex." Orinda was born in 1631 and died in 1664, but, as her poems did not appear until 1662 and her fame belongs to her last years, she may be accounted a Restoration poet. As she wrote only poetry, she really comes outside the scope of this study, but for the sake of her reputation we cannot pass her by. In her own sentiments with regard to her authorship and in the reception accorded to her works we see perfectly mirrored the attitude of the England of her day to the woman writer. Little need be said about her life. She was no court lady but the daughter of a London merchant, who married in 1648 a country gentleman, James Phillips, Esq., of Cardigan Priory. To enliven the tedium of her quiet country life she founded what she called a "Society of

Friendship," whose objects were the discussion of "poetry, religion and the affairs of the heart." It was to the members of this society that her poems were chiefly written and to one especially, a Miss Anne Owen, her "adored Lucasia," did Orinda open her heart—until Lucasia broke the vows of her initiation and married. Finally, against her will, compelled, in fact, by the circulation of a pirated edition of her works, Orinda "upon great persuasion" brought herself to face the ordeal of publication. After this first bold step she went even further. On a visit to Ireland she yielded to the "pressing importunities" of the Earls of Orrery and Roscommon and allowed her translations of *Horace* and *Pompey* to be played upon the Irish stage.

There seems to us nothing in Orinda's works to account for the sensation they created on their first appearance. She was a woman with a genius for friendship, a talent for writing verse, and no sense of humour to restrain her in the expression of her feelings. But, in 1662, her poems were more than poems—they were the work of a woman and therefore an element of the marvellous seemed present in their composition. Orinda herself was diffident enough about her position as an author.[3] "I am so far from expecting applause in anything I scribble that I can hardly expect pardon," she says in her Preface, "and sometimes think that employment so far above my reach and unfit for my sex that I am going to resolve against it for ever." Such excessive modesty was, in the eyes of her critics, becoming to her. Her Preface, in fact, struck exactly the right note. What she would not say of herself the men of letters of the day were only too ready to say for her. In an age when flattery was common, the poets surpassed themselves in eulogizing this Female Poet. Out of many fantastic compliments, one, from Lord Roscommon, may be quoted as a fair sample. This poet proclaims that in the somewhat improbable event of his being surrounded by wild beasts in the desert:

> The magic of Orinda's name
> Not only can their fierceness tame
> But if that mighty name I once rehearse
> They seem submissively to roar in verse[4]

[3] Mrs Katharine Phillips, *Works*. London, 1768. preface.

[4] Sir E. Gosse, *Seventeenth Century Studies*. New York, 1897. (Quoted from Roscommon's *Works*.)

This is the very ecstasy of criticism. Orinda's reputation indeed represents the height of the female poet's fame. Her glory lasted on into the eighteenth century, through which we can trace an Orinda legend: the feminist of that age, when challenged, may reply at once "Have we not Madame Dacier, Anna Von Schurman and the Matchless Orinda?"[5] But no one can mistake the patronage in the panegyrics of the other sex. "Ah! cruel sex, would you depose us, too, in wit?" cries Cowley, but he does not think there is really much danger. "There is no being pleased in their conversation," says a character in one of Mrs Manley's books, discussing women, "without a mixture of the sex, which will still be mingling itself in all we say."[6] There was no being pleased in a woman's work either without some "mixture of the sex", which is certainly present in all her critics have to say about Orinda.

I have dwelt on Mrs Katharine Phillips at a length perhaps disproportionate to her historic importance, because the public attitude to her prepares us for the difficulties ahead when women began to write for a living. The Duchess of Newcastle's position only makes the situation clearer. Margaret Cavendish, Duchess of Newcastle, was born in 1623 and had begun to write in France before she returned to England with the exiled House of Stuart, but, as with Orinda, her fame belongs to the period after the Restoration. Her reputation, however, rests on a different basis from that of Mrs Phillips, for strong disapproval and even ridicule enters into it. She had her panegyrists it is true—witness those two noble collections, the *Letters and Poems in Honour of the Incomparable Princess, Margaret: Duchess of Newcastle*, published in 1676; and a similar volume two years later: *Written by Several Persons of Honour and Learning upon divers important subjects, to the late Duke and Duchess of Newcastle.* Her ingenious method of securing these forced tributes has, however, outlived her; it is possible too that the "persons of honour and learning" were influenced by her rank and by the Duke's fondness for playing the part of Maecenas. John Evelyn at any rate writes one thing to her face[7] and another in

[5] For accounts of Madame Dacier and Anna Von Schurman see Reynolds, *Learned Lady in England.*

[6] Mary de la Riviere Manley, *Adventures of Rivella*. London, 1714.

[7] John Evelyn, *Correspondence* (ed. Bray) p. 668 and *Diary* 1667, May, 30. (see also Pepys's *Diary* for the same day.)

the confessional of his diary where he calls her no longer the wonder of the age but a "mighty pretender to learning, poetry and philosophy."

It was the fact that the Duchess was a pretender to philosophy that was chiefly responsible for the disapproval of the age. Poetry might be considered a not unsuitable accomplishment for women; in this matter the men of Charles II's time would have agreed with Montaigne, who wrote thus of women in 1580:

"What need they more than to live beloved and honoured? . . . . Yet if it offend them to yield us any preheminence and would for curiosity sake have part in bookes also, Poesie is a study fit for their purpose, being a wanton, amusing, subtill, disguised and prating art: all in delight, all in show, like to themselves."[8]

But a woman philosopher was not to be so lightly accepted as a woman poet. We have only to read Fontenelle's *Plurality of Worlds*, published in 1686, to see how public opinion ran on this subject. Fontenelle's Marchioness is the type of woman philosopher the times would have allowed, though even she is cautioned not to talk about what she knows. For her benefit the Cartesian system is "softened" and simplified; for her the "savage nature"[9] of philosophy is changed. She is not given even the dilute science of the Dialogues without something more acceptable to her female mind; a vein of gallantry runs through the philosopher's most serious explanations. But the Duchess was not such a one. She wrote not of the theories of others, "softened," but of the fancies of her own brain. Moreover she did not wait to be pressed and forced into publication. She *insisted* on publishing:

> For had my brain as many fancies in't
> To fill the world, I'd put them all in print—[10]

and in a series of works with such harsh-sounding and unbecoming titles as *Philosophical Fancies* (1653), *Philosophical Letters* (1664), and *Observations upon Experimental Philosophy* (1668) she thrust her opinions upon a scandalised world.

[8] Montaigne (trans. Florio). London, 1898. V, p. 56.

[9] *Sir Isaac Newton's Philosophy Explained, Translated from the Italian of Signor A*. London, 1739. (Trans. Elizabeth Carter from the Italian of Algarotti, *il Newtoniansme per le dame*, Naples, 1737—a work dedicated to Fontenelle.)

[10] For this and succeeding quotations from *Poems and Fancies* and *Philosophical and Physical Opinions* I am indebted to Henry Ten Eyck Perry's *First Duchess of Newcastle* Boston, 1918.

Her fantastic theories do not concern us here. What does concern us is her reception by the public and her own attitude to her authorship. In her Preface to her first published work, *Poems and Fancies* (1653), she goes half way to meet her critics:

"If any do read this book of mine pray be not too severe in your Censures. For, first, I have no Children to employ my care and attendance on: and my Lord's Estate being taken away, had nothing for Housewifery or Thrifty Industry to employ myself in. . . . . Thirdly, you are to spare your severe Censures, I having not so many Years of Experience as will make me a Garland to Crowne my head."

This little appeal, however, did not disarm her readers. Some, like Dorothy Osborne,[11] took the attitude that her book was "ten times more extravagent than her dress" and that there were "many soberer people in Bedlam." Others turned round completely and said no woman could have written such books as "no lady could understand so many hard words."

Against this last aspersion the Duke tried to defend his wife in the epistle prefixed to the 1665 edition of *Philosophical and Physical Opinions*. Here he states in a memorable sentence, a difficulty with which women authors had to contend for years to come. "But here's the crime," he says, "a lady writes them and to intrench so much on the male prerogative is not to be forgiven." In the same work, the Duchess, in her *Epistle to the Two Universities*, comes forward as an early advocate of the emancipation of her sex. She exhorts the universities to encourage the education of women "lest in time we should grow irrational as idiots . . . . for we are kept like birds in cages to hop up and down in our houses"—a remarkable sentiment in 1653, four years before the appearance in English of Anna Von Schurman's *De Ingeniis Muliebris* the first feminist document published in England, nearly forty years before Mary Astell's *Serious Proposal* and over two hundred years before Ibsen's *Doll's House*. Finally, in her Preface to the *Life of the Duke* in 1667, the Duchess reviews her position. She has suffered, she says, from the carping of critics who say she could not have written her books and that they were ill-writ if she had, but she will not allow such as these to drive her into silence. "I

[11] Dorothy Osborne, *Letters* (ed. Parry, 1888) p. 92 and p. iii. For other contemporary opinions of the Duchess see: Pepys, *Diary*, 1667, March 30; April 11; May 1; May 30. Hamilton, *Memoirs of Count Grammont*. London, 1864. p. 135.

matter not the censures of the age," she cries defiantly, "but am, rather, proud of them."

"Mad Madge of Newcastle" cannot be taken as typical of any age. Her unconventionality in dress and behaviour had as much to do with contemporary opinion of her as her singularity in writing books. She had at the same time a safeguard in her rank and birth; a Duchess could—and still can—indulge in vagaries which would not be tolerated in ordinary mortals. But her reputation, taken in conjunction with that of Orinda, does show us what the public would accept and what it would not in the world into which the first professional woman writer was now to be launched.

# PART I

# THE CHANGE IN POSITION OF THE WOMAN NOVELIST, 1688–1797

## CHAPTER I

## "THE FAIR TRIUMVIRATE OF WIT"

### 1. Aphra Behn, 1640–1689

Aphra Behn was the first woman novelist and the first professional woman writer. Her biography has gathered round it a literature of its own.[1] This is not the place to enter into its details. There is reason, however, to believe that she was Aphra Amis and not Aphra Johnson and that her father was John Amis, a man of good family, and not John Johnson, the barber, whose lowly birth has been responsible for the supercilious tone assumed by many of of M^rs^ Behn's critics. She was born in Wye, Kent, in 1640, and made the voyage to Surinam described in *Oroonoko* while she was still a child.

Her father died on the outward voyage and we hear no mention at all of her mother. Under whose care she lived in Surinam and what education she can have acquired there, we do not know. Perhaps, like Oroonoko, she met with a "Frenchman of wit and learning," who taught her his language, for she had a knowledge of French that in later days enabled her to translate Fontenelle and the Abbé Tallemant. That she found means of reading history and romance we can guess from the tales with which she entertained the royal slaves—lives of the Romans for Oroonoko and stories of nuns for Imoinda. Nor were the usual accomplishments of her sex entirely neglected, for she speaks of the "pretty works" which she taught Imoinda and of the flute playing

[1] The following biographies and articles give most of the facts and fictions about M^rs^ Behn:

*Life of M^rs^ Behn written by one of the Fair Sex.* 1696.

*Life of the Incomparable M^rs^ Behn.* Charles Gildon. 1696. (Prefixed to the *Younger Brother.*)

*M^rs^ Behn's Oroonoko* and *M^rs^ Behn's Biography of Fiction.* Ernest Bernbaum. 1913.

*Introduction to Works of M^rs^ Behn.* Montague Summers. 1915.

which charmed the natives of the Indian village. At least she lost nothing in missing the regular education of the girl of her class in England. The schooling which in the sixteen-fifties was considered "fit for young gentlewomen," was no very serious affair, dancing, music, and embroidery being the chief items of the curriculum in the boarding school, as they were in the education conducted in the home. Mrs Bathsua Makin's[2] school at Tottenham High Cross, where Latin, French, and even Hebrew were taught, was the experimental school of that age, to which most parents would hesitate to trust their daughters. Intercourse with the men of different nations who came and went in the West Indies must have done far more to develop the naturally lively wit of Aphra Amis than the society of sober gentlewomen of her own age in a dame's school, and her hunting and fishing expeditions among the vivid beauties of the tropical landscape must have stirred her imagination more than "walking among the shades and groves planted by herself"[3] on her embroidery frame.

She returned to England about 1663 when she married the Dutch merchant Behn. After the death of her husband in 1665 she became involved in a diplomatic mission to Holland, round which much picturesque legend has gathered, but which really seems to have ended disastrously by her being thrown into prison for debts contracted for her country; and it was after her failure as a secret agent that she turned to authorship as a means of self-support. From the *Forced Marriage* in 1670 to the *Emperor of the Moon* in 1687 her plays appeared with regularity and were put on the boards with a fair amount of success. It is probable that in these years she was also experimenting with the novel. From 1687 to 1689 were published all the novels which appeared in her lifetime. Besides her plays and novels she wrote poems and translated from the French. Up to the time of her death in 1689 she was, apparently, constantly at work.

Even from this brief outline it will be seen that her life was a remarkable one. She had experiences which few women of her

[2] Mrs Bathsua Makin (died 1673) was tutor to Princess Elizabeth, daughter of Charles I, and later kept a school, first at Putney then at Tottenham High Cross. With her Prospectus in 1673, she issued an *Essay to Revive the Antient Education of Gentlewomen* which comprises a list of the learned women of the past, an answer to the common objections raised against the learned woman, and a simplified Latin grammar more suited to the comprehension of young ladies.

[3] *Spectator*. Oct. 13, 1714. (No. 606.)

day could have had and which few would have welcomed. She crossed the Atlantic at a time when few of her sex ever crossed the Channel; she hunted tigers amid the vivid tropical scenery of the West Indies. In her connection with the diplomatic service she had opportunities from which Englishwomen even today are excluded. She knew the theatre from behind the scenes, when it was a bold thing for a woman to sit in the audience, masked. That all her experiences were equally desirable, no one can claim. "What Aphra Behn was, we all know," remarks her Victorian biographer, Julia Kavanagh, walking delicately amid the muddy patches of her author's life; and it is almost certain that in the beginning of her career as a dramatist, at least, she did not rely entirely on her pen for self-support. But authorship in the days of the Patron was even more precarious as a living than it is today, and, if Aphra Behn lived for a time as a kept mistress, she had too much character to degenerate into a mere woman of the town and hanger-on of the theatres. She must have been conscious of having faced realities from which the generality of her sex were sheltered, and this consciousness gave her power. One wonders what she thought of the Orindas of the time.

The way to success, for Mrs Behn, was to write like a man, and her chosen career laid her open to all the buffets of the playwright's life, as lived by the men of the Restoration. Stage history, at this time, is a record of personal jealousies, petty squabbles, attacks and counter attacks. Mrs Behn was there to be the butt of any little lampooner with a grudge against her or her associates; or of the Puritan moralist who could make an example of her all the better because she was a woman. She had to face a man's difficulties and a woman's, too. Were her plays a failure, "a woman had writ them." Were they successful, they must have been written by a man. In the Post-script to the *Rover* we find her defending herself against a "malitious" charge of plagiarism.[4] The audiences, no less than the critics, were prejudiced against her sex. In the "Epistle to the Reader" prefixed to the *Dutch Lover* she speaks of a long lither "thing," who tried to influence the first-night crowd, by telling them "they were to expect a woful play, God damn him, for it was a woman's"—and to him and his kind she replies with vigour. Men's great advantage over women,

[4] There is a tradition that Edward Ravenscroft, lawyer and dramatist, was responsible for some of Mrs Behn's plays.

she says, is in Learning, and in plays there is no need of Learning. "We all know well that the immortal Shakespeare's Plays (who was not guilty of much more of this than often falls to woman's share) have better pleased the world than Johnson's works, though, by the way 'tis said that Benjamin was no such Rabbi neither, for I am informed that his learning was but Grammar high: (sufficient indeed to rob Sallust of his best orations) . . . . . Then for their musty rules of Unity and God knows what beside, if they meant anything they are intelligible and practicable by a woman."[5]

She was a bold woman, indeed, who could speak thus of Jonson and the Unities, and it is this fearlessness in giving her own opinions which marks her out at a time when most women had no opinions to give. *Oroonoko* is an outspoken criticism of British policy in the West Indian Colonies. The natives represent man in the state of innocence; the white men are distinguished by cruelty and breaches of faith. She is not afraid to show up the characters of individuals. Byam, the deputy governor, is "a fellow whose character is not fit to be mentioned with the worst of the slaves";[6] Bannister, a member of the Council, is "a fellow of absolute barbarity and fit to execute any villainy, but rich."[7] The whole group, in fact, of his Majesty's servants in Surinam she dismisses as "such notorious villains as Newgate never transported."[8] Perhaps the readers of the age were too much interested in the fate of the Royal Slave to be alive to the implications of the social and political questions and conditions raised by the author—we have no record of the attitude of the public to *Oroonoko* except that several editions were called for. But more interesting to us than the romantic story is the fact that here was a woman writing of the "natural man" before Rousseau, of slavery before Wilberforce, and claiming the right to say what she thought, before women were out of their leading strings.

M^rs^ Behn's reputation has suffered from the superior morality of her critics. "The Boards how loosely does Astraea tread,"[9]

[5] Aphra Behn, *Works*. 1915. (ed. Montague Summers.) Vol. I, p. 224.

[6] *Ibid.*, V, p. 194.

[7] *Ibid.*, V, p. 207.

[8] *Ibid.*, V, p. 200.

[9] Pope, *Epistle to Augustus*, l. 290.
The boards how loosely does Astraea tread
Who fairly puts all characters to bed.

they cry, forgetting that Astraea was writing to please the audiences of the Restoration and that, had she trod the boards less "loosely" she would not have been suffered to tread them so long, nor to the accompaniment of such applause. "The inveterate coarseness of her mind sullied Aphra Behn's noblest gifts,"[10] writes Julia Kavanagh, after trying to say a good word for "poor Aphra Behn." "Beauty, sincerity, wit, an eloquent tongue and a ready pen, perished in the wreck of all that is delicate and refined in women." But delicacy and refinement would not have carried her very far in the Restoration theatre. M^rs Behn has come to be a symbol of all that is unwomanly and undesirable, the disgrace of her sex rather than its glory. "From them that use men thus, Good Lord deliver us"—for it is hopeless to approach M^rs Behn from the modern standpoint of decency. What her contemporaries thought of her, we know too little. Pepys, curiously enough, does not mention her name, though so habitual a theatregoer can hardly have missed seeing her plays, and, where Pepys is silent, one is at a loss where to look for the current opinions of the age. The Restoration had no Spectator nor Sylvanus Urban to whom we can turn for evidence, and there is no record of the opinions concerning her held by Dryden or by Otway and the rest of the leading dramatists of the time, though she must have been acquainted with them in her theatrical life. That she had her detractors proves nothing but that she was a public character. The mere fact that she is coupled with Dryden in one attack[11] is enough to show that these contemporary lampoons had no critical value.

She had also her eulogists. The minor poets of the age, seeking, like all their race, to hand on their names to posterity by attaching them to a greater than themselves, were an admiring chorus on the publication of the *Lovers' Watch* and the *Poems*.[12] Charles Cotton contributes a poem to the "Divine Astraea" and Nahum Tate to the "Incomparable Author". "To the Most ingenious Astraea"; "Upon the Incomparable Astraea"; "To the Lovely, Witty Astraea" are some of the titles of the verses in these collections.

[10] Julia Kavanagh, *English Women of Letters*. London, 1863. Vol. I, p. 7.

[11] *A Satyr on Modern Translators* by M^r P———r. 1684. Included in Prior's *Works*. 1905.

[12] Aphra Behn, *Works*. Vol. VI. (In *Poems* prefixd to *La Monstre*, 1684, and to *Poems upon Several Occasions*, 1684.)

> The pride of Greece we now outrival'd see
> Greece boasts one Sappho, two Orindas we,

writes Nahum Tate and the rest are merely a variation on this rather obvious theme. Astraea is the "young succeeded Phoenix" who arises from Orinda's "spicy obsequies"; she is the female laureate who receives the chaplet from Orinda's brows. How Mrs Phillips would have blushed at the connection! The verses are not criticism, of course. Much of their language belongs to the common stock of compliments to women.

> I am too dull to write but I can love,

says Cotton and a certain J. W. echoes Cowley on Orinda when he complains

> To wound with Beauty's fighting on the square
> But to o'ercome in wit too, is not fair.

But neither these nor the attacks of the satirists may be taken as a reflection of contemporary opinion. They are an expression of personal feeling and an example of a literary convention.

If the *Life of Mrs Behn written by one of the Fair Sex* and Charles Gildon's *Life of the Incomparable Mrs Behn*, both of which appeared in 1696, are responsible for perpetuating the romantic fictions that gathered round her name, at least one need not doubt their candour in what they record of the author's personality; and one may well believe that Mrs Behn impressed the age as a woman of wit and vivacity, an excellent conversationalist, and a plain dealer. We have her picture by Lely to bear out this impression—the portrait of a fine-looking woman, with the full lips of the pleasure lover and bold dark eyes that stare the world in the face.

Her ghost makes an interesting appearance half a century after her death in a vision called the "Apotheosis of Milton", which begins in the May number of the *Gentleman's Magazine* for 1738 and drags its slow length along through that year and the next. The author, having been compelled to spend a night in Westminster Abbey, finds he has arrived in time to see the initiation of Milton into the company of the Great, and, under the guidance of the Genius of the Abbey, he watches the filling up of the assembly. Between Cowley and Prior comes Aphra Behn.

"But observe that Lady," says the guide[13] . . . . . "How much Fire in her Eye! What a passionate Expression in her Motions;

[13] *Gentleman's Magazine.* 1738. Vol. VIII, p. 469.

And how much Assurance in her Features! Observe what an indignant Look she bestows on the President who is telling her that none of her Sex has any right to a Seat there. How she throws her Eyes about to see if she can find out any one of the Assembly who enclines to take her part. No! not one stirs; they who are enclined in her Favour are overawed and the rest shake their Heads and how she flings out of the Assembly. That extraordinary Woman is Afra Behn." If she was rejected by the assembly, at least she showed herself a person to be reckoned with and the very fact that she was honoured with a tomb in Westminster Abbey shows that to her contemporaries she was no unimportant figure.

M^rs^ Behn seems to have been less hampered by the traditions of her sex than any woman author for years to come. She had seen more of the world than many men; in competition with men, without much education and without money or position, she had won her way into public life. Therefore she did not find it necessary to come before her readers with creeping apologies for the liberty she was taking in attempting tasks "above her sex." She left the world to judge whether such things were above her sex or not; and it is to the honour of the society of Charles II's reign that it was never willing to let wit go unrecognized. No woman since her day has occupied quite the same position. Women on the whole have not succeeded in the writing of drama. "The method of the theatre," as M^r^ James Agate says, "is the method of the town cryer," and this is not the method of women. There have been good plays by women, it is true, but it is not women who make the theatre. Indeed, one thinks of no woman since M^rs^ Behn who has held the stage as she did with a long run of popular plays. The fact that she wrote plays that pleased and novels that sold is of more importance in the history of Feminism than all the flattering verses addressed to the "Matchless Orinda."

M^rs^ Behn in her lifetime occupied an isolated position as a "female wit", nor at her death does there appear anyone on whom she might let fall her mantle. In the year 1696, however, three new women dramatists appeared before the public and, in the following year, in a play called the *Female Wits*, by a certain W. M., all three are pilloried. Of the three leading characters in the play only one concerns us here. "Calista"—Miss Catherine Trotter,[14]

[14] Catherine Trotter, M^rs^ Cockburn (1679–1749) whose first tragedy *Agnes de Castro* in 1696 won her the approval of Congreve and Farquhar. M^rs^ Manley hailed

a young lady of noble family—received attention enough from her age to make up for that which she has been denied by posterity. Her true fame belongs to a later date when she became Mrs Cockburn and a combatant in religious and philosophical warfare. "Mrs Welffed" who was Mrs Pix,[15] wife of a merchant tailor of London and a writer of poor tragedies is still less important. But Marsilia, in whom the audiences of 1697 might recognize Mrs Mary de la Riviere Manley, author of two plays which had failed and a mistress of Sir Thomas Skipworth of Drury Lane Theatre, was destined to become a notorious figure in Anne's reign, and the successor of Mrs Behn as a writer of fiction.

## 2. MARY DE LA RIVIERE MANLEY, 1672–1724

Mary de la Riviere Manley came, like Mrs Behn, of a good stock, as the daughter of Sir Roger Manley, Governor of Guernsey, himself something of a man of letters. She started life with the handicap of being "of indifferent beauty between two sisters perfectly handsome," but she seems to have made up for this initial disadvantage by superior wits, for we never hear again of the beautiful sisters. Of the education which she received, first under the care of a "severe governess," then of an old "out-of-fashion aunt" with whom she lived after her father's death, we know little enough; but, beyond the fact that she was sent for a time to learn French from a Huguenot minister, we do not gather that there was any plan or method in it. Indeed, it is very probable that she spent most of her time in reading the French romances which she found in her aunt's house and in writing verses and letters. We have a general impression that she passed an unhappy, neglected childhood and received little either of guidance or affection from her relations, and it was probably with a desire to escape from this atmosphere that she allowed herself to be tricked into a marriage with her cousin, John Manley of Truro. The

---

her as "Nature's third start in favour of our sex"—Orinda and Mrs Behn being Nature's first and second "starts" respectively. Beginning with a *Defence of the Essay of Human Understanding* in 1701, she published a series of controversial works at intervals during the rest of her life and her *Works* were published in 1751.

[15] Mrs Mary Pix (1666–1720) wrote, between the years 1696 and 1706, five tragedies and one comedy all of which were played. Her name appears in the original *Dunciad* (Pope's *Works*. Elwin & Courthope. IV, p. 294) but was struck out in the final version.

marriage was a false one, and Mr Manley chose the moment of the birth of her child to desert his wife, having acquainted her with the fact that "His Lady" was yet living. Mrs Manley, now stranded in London, did not choose to return to her family but lived for a time under the protection of the Duchess of Cleveland until, through some obscure scandal, she lost the interest of that influential lady. It was then, in 1696, that she turned to the theatre as a livelihood and produced her first two plays, *The Royal Mischief* and the *Lost Lover*. If these two plays did not bring in her living, her connection with the theatre did, for she became mistress to Sir Thomas Skipworth of Drury Lane and for a time we hear no more of her. In 1705, reduced again to the necessity of writing, she published her history of *Queen Zarah and the Zarazians*, and from this time to her death in 1724 she is well known to the public as an author.

In *Queen Zarah* she struck a note which pleased the public ear. The whole world loves a scandal and scandals about "persons of quality of both sexes" have a special appeal at all times. In spite of the author's solemn assertion that the history was a fiction, "that there is no such country in the world as Albigion nor any such person now living, nor ever was, as Zarah, no one could have had much difficulty in recognizing the Duchess of Marlborough in the principal character and everybody but the Duchess must have enjoyed it. When in the year 1709 she continued her "secret memoirs," in the *New Atlantis*, she found fame, indeed, but a fame that brought her into contact with the law against libel. The office of Court Scandalmonger was not evidently to be licensed, for we find recorded in Luttrell's *Diary* for November 1, 1709 that "on this day the printer and publisher of the *New Atlantis* were examined touching the author, Mrs Manley: they were discharged but she remains in custody." Another statement for November 5 tells us that "Mrs Manley, the author of the *New Atlantis*, is admitted to Bayl." How in the end she was discharged with a caution, she tells us in *Rivella*, and it is probable that the warning of the court had some effect; for though the volumes of the *Atlantis* already written appeared, and the whole ran into several editions, the secret history included in *Rivella* in 1714 is comparatively tame and *The Power of Love* in 1720 is pure fiction. After *The Power of Love* we hear no more of her. She died in 1724 at the house of the John Barber whose "impartiall history" was written by Curll, and with whom she had lived for the last years of her life.

Mrs Manley, like Mrs Behn, served her literary apprenticeship in the theatres, but this was a mere incident in her life. That she succeeded as a writer of fiction where she failed as a dramatist is a sign of the times. The drama of the Restoration was long past its heyday, and a long reign of dullness was beginning for the English theatre. The reform of theatres, following Collier's attack in his *Short View of the Stage* in 1698, might have made it more possible for women to write plays as it made it more possible for them to watch them; for, as Cibber tells us, "indecencies were no longer writ and by degrees the fair sex came again to fill the boxes on the first day of a new comedy without fear or censure."[16] But the truth was that neither the "non-juring clergyman" Collier, nor the body of respectable citizens behind him, were satisfied with the mere censorship of plays; they would have abolished the theatre root and branch, like the Puritans, and, though they did not get their way, they managed to convey a powerful impression of disapproval. Besides this, the impulse which had made Restoration drama was dying. Little was left for the reformers to reform. The reign of Anne was not an inspiring age for the dramatist, either man or woman, and though some women such as Mrs Pix and Mrs Centlivre[17] went on writing for the stage under such difficult conditions, Mrs Manley chose the wiser part in preferring fiction. The eighteenth century is the age of the reader rather than of the theatregoer, and the reading he chose was the novel, the newspaper, and the periodical essay. Therefore, the writer with his way to make, became novelist, journalist, or political pamphleteer, and Mrs Manley in her time was all three.

Mrs Behn, we feel, would have been a writer in any case, but Mrs Manley in easier circumstances, in spite of undoubted talents, would probably not have written at all. Obviously she was under no delusion about Art or the high calling of the author; her critical sense was sufficiently developed to make her realize that most of her work was of the class of what today we call "potboilers." In

[16] Colley Cibber, *An Apology for his Life*. Everyman's Edition. p. 143.

[17] Suzanna Centlivre (1680–1723) produced between the years 1703–1722 seventeen popular comedies. Her works were collected and published in 1761, with a defense of female authors by an anonymous woman writer. Mrs Centlivre's name also occurred in the *Dunciad* in the passage noted above.

the *New Atlantis*, with reference to a poem she quotes by "Colonel Finch's lady," better known as Lady Winchilsea, she says, "I presume she's one of the few that write out of pleasure and not necessity. By that means it's her own fault if she publish anything but what's good."[18] And there must have been moments when she envied such elegant amateurs as "Ardelia," writing her poems, as fancy took her, in the calm seclusion of Eastwell. That the life of the professional author was anything but calm, we have not only Mrs Manley's life to witness, but the lives of the greatest men of the age. Steele came in contact with the libel laws no less than the author of the *Atlantis*, and Swift did hackwork for Harley as Mrs Manley did hackwork for Swift. Literature, in the reign of Anne, went hand in hand with politics, and the great patrons were the leaders of the State. A ready pen could bring a man political preferment, but it had to be used thereafter in the service of Party. The first necessity, for the author, was to make up his mind whether he were Whig or Tory and choose his patron accordingly. Since Mrs Manley was a Tory, she appealed to Swift, for whom she wrote pamphlets and edited *Examiners*, and who used his influence in return to try to get her a pension "or reward for her service in the cause, by writing her *Atlantis* and prosecution upon it."[19] It seems curious to us to think of the *Atlantis* as a service to any cause, and that a man like Swift could so regard it is an interesting light on the methods of authors and politicians of the day.

Yet it is probable that the age regarded Mrs Manley chiefly in the light of a party writer. The readers of the time preferred truth like lies to lies like truth, and liked to think there were facts behind her stories. That she had her own views on fiction we know from the preface to *Zarah*, which is an excellent criticism of the faults of the romances. For a moment we feel the author is coming forward as a reformer of the English novel; but the history which follows soon dispels any such idea. It was only in her prefaces that she could afford to indulge in theories and let us see the writer she might have been. Her great asset, as she well knew, was in the store of gossip she had collected in the household of the Duchess

[18] *New Atlantis*. 1709. Vol. I, p. 186. Lady Winchilsea's *Poems* were not published until 1713, when a volume under the name of Ardelia appeared, but Mrs Manley's reference shows that some of the verse must have been known in 1709.

[19] Swift, *Journal to Stella*. June 30, 1711.

of Cleveland and added to by her own observation and invention; and, in making use of this to blacken one party, she contrived to be of service to the other. The fact that here was a woman taking part in politics and incidentally becoming the first woman journalist seems an important one to us as we look back over two hundred years of the history of women. Probably, however, it meant little to the times she lived in. She was merely another tool of the party, and it may never have leaked out that the author of the *Atlantis* had a hand in Tory pamphlets and periodicals. Nothing could be more casual than Swift's reference to the account of Guiscard's attempt on Harley's life, which she wrote up for him. "I had not time to do it myself," he says, "so I sent my hints to the author of the *Atlantis* and she has cooked it up into a sixpenny pamphlet in her own style."[20] This "I had not time to do it myself," from Swift, is the measure of M[rs] Manley's importance to the Government.

In attempting to judge of M[rs] Manley's reputation in her day, we can be certain at the outset that, whatever people thought of her, they read her. The mere fact that the *Tatler* and *Spectator* can refer so often to the "author of the *Atlantis*," without any explanation, shows that she was sufficiently well known to their readers to be taken for granted. The *New Atlantis* is included in the representative selection that is Leonora's Library,[21] and, soon after its publication, we find Lady Mary Wortley Montagu enquiring for the second part of it. Although by the time Charlotte Lennox wrote, this "charmingly pretty book" is relegated to the shelves of milliners and the like, in M[rs] Manley's own time there is no doubt that it was read by high and low. But with all this popularity, we miss in the reception accorded to the author of the *Atlantis*, the excitement created by Orinda and even by M[rs] Behn. "Epicene" had the distinction of an attack in the *Tatler*, but no one comes forward to call her "divine," "incomparable," "Albion and her sex's grace." It was reserved for her, indeed, to write her own eulogy. Perhaps this is because the "scribbling woman" is no longer a curiosity; perhaps it was that M[rs] Manley's character was too notorious to encourage the usual strain of compliment. Or it may be that the age had lost its courtliness and that the attitude toward women was changing.

[20] *Ibid.* April 15, 1711.

[21] *Spectator*, April 12, 1711. (No. 37.)

We have, indeed, to understand the general attitude of the times towards women, before we can appreciate its attitude towards the particular woman in question. We might imagine that because there was a woman ruler, female influence might be prevalent in the higher circles of society. But, in point of fact, the age of Anne was very far from petticoat government. It was essentially masculine and man-governed. The coffee-house, not the Court, was the centre of Town life, and, from the society of coffee-houses women were excluded. For the men of the time the coffee-house was the world; it was the senate where they settled the affairs of the nation; it was the Exchange where they settled their own; it was, moreover, the club in which they passed their hours of leisure. Here, over their coffee in the morning, they could discuss questions of literature and politics while my lady of fashion lay abed and drank her chocolate, and here, in the evening, they could grow convivial over their bottle while their wives at home perplexed their wits over basset and ombre. Men sought the company of men because the society of women afforded them no intellectual companionship, yet there is no evidence that they tried to change this state of affairs. Even Pepys, who looked upon his wife as his chattel, had stayed at home, occasionally, to read to her, or teach her astronomy; but Addison, though he professed to educate his women readers through the medium of his papers, still gave his days and nights to the society of men. And, in the end, what does all the Spectator's prattle about the fair sex amount to? Addison at least can never be quite serious in talking to the ladies.

"I have often wondered," he says, "that learning is not thought a proper ingredient in the education of a woman of quality or fortune. Since they have the same improvable minds as the male part of the species, why should they not be cultivated by the same methods?"[22] Here, we might think, is a feminist, if not a very ardent one; but the next paragraph spoils the impression when he goes on to describe the picture of Lady Lizard's family combining their jam-making with readings from the *Plurality of Worlds*. "It was very entertaining to me," he writes, "to see them dividing their speculations between jellies and stars and making a sudden transition from the sun to an apricot or from the Copernican sys-

[22] *Guardian*. September 8, 1713. (No. 155.)

tem to the figure of a cheesecake." He has no objection to a little learning in women—it might keep them out of mischief, indeed—but it must not interfere with the proper duties of the sex. "Female virtues are of a domestic turn. The family is the proper province for the private woman to shine in."[23] The woman who professes an interest in politics comes in for her share of gentle ridicule. He pictures the disorder of a household ruled by an angry stateswoman or, worse still, the havoc which excess of party zeal can work in a pretty face. "Indeed, I never knew a party-woman that kept her beauty for a twelfth-month,"[24] he says, sure of the efficacy of an appeal to feminine vanity. Woman is to Addison "a beautiful romantic animal, that may be adorned with furs and feathers, pearls and diamonds, ores and silks."[25] She speaks, moves, and smiles "with regard to that other half of reasonable creatures"; her thoughts are "ever turned upon appearing aimiable to the other sex."[26] And he is anxious that she should keep her beauty and romance, and afraid of any encroachment on the ways of the opposite sex that might destroy her charm. "I think it absolutely necessary," he says, "to keep up the partition between the two sexes and to take notice of the smallest encroachments that the one makes on the other."[27] And Addison is not singular in his attitude; it is no uncommon one today, among middle-aged men, or even in the young man bred in the public schools—and without sisters. He has chosen, moreover, the very way to make his assertions about women incontrovertible. We may be roused by this gentle, mocking patronage—how women like Mary Astell must have writhed under it!—but Addison will have the laugh of us in the end.

Steele is more truly a lover of the sex than Addison, as he is warmer natured altogether. In the company of women he is less aloof, less completely master of himself; hence, his raillery is easier to meet. He was known, even to his own age, as a writer of charming love-letters: "I wish you would learn of M^r Steele to write to your wife," writes Lady Mary to the ungallant M^r Wortley Montagu. His praise of the Lady Elizabeth Hastings that "to

[23] *Spectator.* June 2, 1711. (No. 81.)
[24] *Spectator.* May 5, 1711. (No. 57.)
[25] *Tatler.* Jan. 5, 1709. (No. 116.)
[26] *Spectator.* July 17, 1712. (No. 433.)
[27] *Spectator.* July 19, 1712. (No. 435.)

love her is a liberal education" is become a classic. Steele is sincere enough in offering his love and services to women: one does not feel with him as with many men, that his compliments have risen automatically to his lips, because he is talking to creatures who expect it of him. But, while Addison talks to a woman from above her head, and Steele is at her feet, the result is the same in the end, for neither of them meets her on the level. When they want to improve her mind they give her the "Ladies' Library," a compilation of all the moralizings on women of their own and the last century. They talk to her of the responsibilities of a wife and mother, and of the care of her soul. But they do not give her books that are books, nor do they suggest anything that will stimulate her intellect.

From the *Spectator*, in which the current opinion of the age of Anne is epitomized, we come back to M^rs^ Manley. We can imagine what would have been the Spectator's opinion of her, even had their relations not been complicated by political feeling. Her character was against her in the first place and there was no obligation to treat her with respect. Public School morality in England today makes a rigid distinction between the woman one may marry and the woman with whom one may amuse oneself. M^rs^ Manley belonged to the latter class. Where Swift in writing of her to Stella uses the words "one of her sort," he is placing her, morally and socially. Addison laughs openly when he mentions her name. Describing an adventure of his with an invisible ring which took him by night into the bedchambers of London, he adds, at the end of his tale, "I resolved to send it to my loving friend, the author of the *Atlantis*, to furnish a new Secret History of Secret Memoirs";[28] or again in his paper on nomenclators, when he suggests[29] a candidate for the new and useful office of Nomenclatress and enumerates her qualifications, he gives, as a final testimonial to her knowledge of the private history of London and Westminster, that she is a near kinswoman of the author of the *Atlantis*. Addison was a Whig, and M^rs^ Manley a Tory in any case—he sneers at her tattling and she retaliates by decrying his calling of "Idle Spectator"[30]—but his attitude to her is more fundamental than that of a political enemy. To him she was just a

[28] *Tatler*. Nov. 11, 1710. (No. 249.)
[29] *Guardian*. July 14, 1713. (No. 107.)
[30] *New Atlantis*. Vol. III.

scurrilous, scribbling woman, not important enough to matter, but good enough to get a laugh out of.

With Steele M^rs^ Manley had rather special relations. According to her own account in Book I of the *Atlantis*, she had been of service to him in his early life and attacked him under the name of "Monsieur L'Ingrate" because he did not come forward to help her in the time of her distress. Incidentally, this passage contains an acute criticism of Steele's literary style. Two attacks in the "*Tatlers*" of 1709—probably by Swift but attributed by M^rs^ Manley to Steele—embittered her still further, and, in the ironical dedication of Book III to Isaac Bickerstaffe, and the conversation between Steele and M^rs^ Tofts in Book IV, she continues to harp on his ingratitude. In 1713, over the Dunkirk question, there was a further passage of arms, but, when her play *Lucius* appeared in 1717, there is an apology for her past conduct from the author, and the Prologue is written by her old enemy. This quarrel, though it typifies literary relationships as they often were at the time, and shows how women as well as men were liable to be embroiled in them, rather obscures than throws light on Steele's opinion of M^rs^ Manley. That Steele behaved throughout with tolerance and true chivalry is only an instance of his general attitude toward women. All we learn from the incident is that in some way she was able to serve Steele in his youth, and that he had a sufficient respect for her not to take advantage of her position to abuse her, even when she abused him.

Swift was M^rs^ Manley's patron. One does not think of Swift in connection with women as one does of M^r^ Spectator. He thought Addison was wasting his time on trivialities when he talked of patches and petticoats; we see it from his remark to Steele, "I will not meddle with the Spectator: let him fair-sex it to the world's end,"[31] and women are crowded out of his own familiar letters to a woman by the serious affairs of the nation. He felt towards women as he felt towards men: "I heartily detest the animal called man," he says, "though I heartily love John, Peter, Thomas and so forth," and in the same way he heartily loved only Stella and Vanessa and had no use for womankind in general. To him M^rs^ Manley was a poor author in need of help, and to all such, whether men or women, Swift was ready to give the assistance he

[31] Swift, *Journal to Stella*. Feb. 8, 1711–12.

could. "I gave an account of sixty guineas I had collected and am to give them away to two Authors tomorrow and Lord Treasurer has promised me a hundred pounds to reward some others . . . . I was to see a poor poet, one M^r^ Diaper in a nasty garret, very sick. I gave him twenty guineas from Lord Bolingbroke and disposed the other sixty to two other authors."[32] Such an extract from his *Journal* shows how Swift used his influence with Harley and St. John on behalf of the more unfortunate members of his craft. M^rs^ Manley was only another Diaper in his eyes. That he had no very high opinion of her we gather as much from his chance references to her as from his attacks in the *Tatler*. He laughs at her style and spelling. But that he did not despise her abilities is shown, equally plainly, by the fact that he trusted her with work of some importance: gave her not only the writing up of the facts of the Guiscard case, but also the editing of the *Examiner*. Of all her great contemporaries, Swift treated M^rs^ Manley most like a man: there is no "mixture of the sex" in his dealings with her. Her relations with Swift mark the advancement of the woman author more, indeed, than does the widespread popularity of the *Atlantis*.

That M^rs^ Manley was a great writer or an admirable character, no one could pretend. She is a less attractive figure than M^rs^ Behn, whose adventurous life gives her a glamour that M^rs^ Manley lacks and who is besides a woman of greater spirit and keener intellect. But M^rs^ Manley, joining in the literary and political warfare of the day, sallying forth to attack Addison and Steele, and slinging wildly at all "persons of quality of both sexes," is at least to be admired for her courage. She forced herself upon the notice of the great men of the age. The very number of times the *Atlantis* is referred to by her contemporaries goes for something, regardless of the tone in which they speak of it. When the young lord in the *Rape of the Lock* at the glorious moment of his triumph casts about for symbols of perpetuity to describe his enduring fame he thinks of the *Atlantis*. His name will be remembered

> While fish in streams or birds delight in air
> Or in a coach and six the British fair,
> As long as the "Atlantis" shall be read—[33]

[32] *Ibid.* Feb. 12, 1713.

[33] Pope, *Works*. Elwin and Courthope. Vol. II, p. 165. (*Rape of the Lock*. ll. 161–3.)

The *Atlantis* is not read nowadays—its popularity did not live as long as the coach and six—but its author is still famous for the impression she made on her own age.

### 3. Eliza Haywood, 1693–1756

A few years before the death of M^rs^ Manley, there appeared in the *Postboy* for January 7, 1721, the following notice:

"Whereas Elizabeth Haywood, Wife of the Reverend M^r^ Valentine Haywood, eloped from him her Husband on Saturday the 26 of November, last past, and went away without his Knowledge and Consent: This is to give Notice to all persons in general, That if any one shall trust her, either with Money or Goods, or if she shall contract Debts of any kind whatsoever, the said M^r^ Haywood will not pay the same."[34]

This Elizabeth, or Eliza, Haywood would have been recognized by contemporary readers of this announcement as the author of a popular novel called *Love in Excess*, which had appeared in 1719. She may have been known in other capacities, also, for she had appeared as an actress on one occasion at least, in Shadwell's version of *Timon*, when it was produced at Dublin in 1715; and if she was, indeed, Sappho of the *Tatler*[35] she must have attracted public attention earlier than this. But, today, we know very little of the early life of the lady in question. All that is on record is that Eliza Fowler, daughter of a London shopkeeper, married, while she will still in her teens, the Reverend Valentine Haywood, author of a few forgotten theological works; and the next intimation we have is that she is running away from him. This break with her husband is the beginning of M^rs^ Haywood's activity as a writer.

Later in her career, when she is looking back and moralizing in the *Female Spectator* over her own experience, M^rs^ Haywood speaks of the round of pleasures and "promiscuous diversions," in which she indulged in her youth. One wonders how she managed to lead so gay a life with a narrow orthodox clergyman for a husband; still more, how the Reverend Valentine Haywood came to allow his young wife to flaunt herself on the boards of the Smock Alley Playhouse. It looks as though her elopement from him was only the climax of a series of attempts on the part of a high-

[34] Quoted by G. F. Whicher in his *Life and Romances of M^rs^ Eliza Haywood.* 1915. p. 3.

[35] *Tatler.* 1708–9. (No. 6 and No. 40.)

spirited woman to assert herself. Elsewhere, in a letter to Curll, included in the *Female Dunciad*, she speaks of the "little inadvertencies of her early life."[36] This confession from herself, together with Pope's reference to the "two babes of love,"[37] which Curll backed up with his not very trustworthy evidence that they were the children of a poet and a bookseller, suggest that Eliza's character was not always highly moral. But we have only vague hints and unsubstantiated slanders from which to reconstruct her private life, and we have to remember that the mere fact that she was a woman author, a successor of the infamous M^rs^ Manley, an associate of the not over respectable society of the theatres and of Grub Street, was enough to get her an undesirable reputation.

It is probable that when she cut herself off from her husband, M^rs^ Haywood felt fairly confident of her ability to earn her living as a writer. Her little experience of the stage gave her the courage to offer her services to Rich, then owner of the Lincoln's Inn Theatre, and the announcement of her first play, *The Fair Captive*, occurring only a few months after the Reverend Valentine's advertisement, comes with the effect of a counterchallenge to her husband. The popularity of *Love in Excess*, however, gave her a better start in her professional career than her experience as an actress. Her dramatic work, like M^rs^ Manley's, is unimportant, but right up to her death she was a well-known novelist.

It would be tedious and unnecessary here to make a catalogue of all her works. She produced over fifty of the fictitious tales of various kinds that we may loosely class as novels. Some of these, *Love in Excess* and all its train, are pure romances of the type of M^rs^ Behn's stories and the seven novels of M^rs^ Manley's *Power of Love*. Some are secret histories of the type of the *Atlantis*—notably the famous *Court of Carimania*, which brought her more enemies than she knew how to cope with. The best of them, like *Betsy Thoughtless* and *Jemmy and Jenny Jessamy*, are domestic novels of the type which came into fashion after *Pamela*. Besides her plays and romances, M^rs^ Haywood wrote essays, letters, moral tracts,

[36] *Female Dunciad*, 1729; a compilation by Curll issued in reply to the *Dunciad* and containing a story by M^rs^ Haywood originally sent to Curll for another purpose and included in the attack on Pope without her knowledge. See Pope's note to the *Dunciad*. (Pope *Works*. Elwin and Courthope. IV, p. 141.)

[37] *Dunciad*, II, l. 158. (Elwin and Courthope. IV, p. 282.)

and translated from the French. In 1744 she started the popular *Female Spectator*, which she brought out monthly for two years, herself the "onlie begetter" of it. In 1746, from August to October, she produced a weekly paper, the *Parrot*. She was, moreover, for part of the time her own publisher, for in her *Virtuous Villager*, in 1742, appears an advertisement for "new books sold by Eliza Haywood, Publisher at the sign of Fame in Covent Garden." From 1719 to her death in 1756, hardly half a dozen years go by without some new work from the pen of Mrs Haywood. At one period of her life, about the year 1724, she was writing at the rate of a novel a month.

Many who have not read a line of Mrs Haywood's own work have seen her name in a footnote to the *Dunciad*,[38] and her novels on the back of the ass which appears as the frontispiece. Her relations with Pope form a turning point in Mrs Haywood's life. Before 1728, in the years of her greatest activity, when amorous novel after amorous novel came from her pen, we gather that she was a popular author. The first collected edition of her works, in 1724, was ushered in by the usual chorus of minor poets. Richard Savage protests that her "soul-thrilling accents" have brought tears to his eyes; a poem "by an unknown hand" tells how its author was "an atheist to love's power declared" until Mrs Haywood's mastery of the tender passion converted him. James Sterling proclaims her as "Born to delight as to reform the age." The number of the editions of her novels which were called for is a more substantial evidence of her popularity; and we have an indication of the fact that her name was a useful one to the bookseller, in its appearance in big print on the title page of the *Pleasant and Delightful History of Gillian of Croyden*,[39] a work in which she had no concern, but which was advertised as "after the same method as those celebrated novels, by Mrs ELIZA HAYWOOD." Had she contented herself with the exercise of her power "to command the throbbing heart, the wat'ry eye" she might have enjoyed this reputation to the end. But she aspired to write the *Atlantis* of her age and, as Mrs Manley's fate should have taught her, writers of secret histories can enjoy only a dangerous success. She began by alienating her former friend, Richard Savage, by an attack on his mistress in *Memoirs of a Certain Island Adjacent*

[38] *Ibid.*, IV, p. 141. (See also frontispiece of same volume.)

[39] G. F. Whicher, *Mrs Eliza Haywood*. p. 128.

*to Utopia*, and the bard who had sung her praises now called her "A cast-off dame" and "a printer's drudge." But the *Court of Carimania* brought down upon her the wrath of a greater than Savage. For the Court of Carimania is the Richmond court of George II, and two of the characters, Mrs Bellenden and Mrs Howard, happened to be friends of Pope. Therefore Mrs Haywood went into the *Dunciad*.

The *Dunciad* was Pope's means of wiping off personal scores. The fact that its characters change according to the author's latest antipathy show that it was a relief to temporary spite, and, had Mrs Haywood not given the author cause for annoyance just at that time, she might not have found a place in the poem at all. As it is, under cover of the moral purpose of chastising the "shameless scribblers . . . . who in libellous Memoirs and Novels reveal the foibles and misfortunes of both sexes, to the ruin of public fame or disturbance of private happiness,"[40] Pope set out to ruin the public fame and disturb the private happiness of Mrs Haywood, by giving to "Eliza" the most offensive place in his book. How well he succeeded is shown by the subsequent change in the reputation of the "great arbitress of passion." Mrs Haywood seems to have gone completely out of fashion. For the next ten years she was driven to hackwork, chiefly to translations, for her livelihood. *Evoaai*, her last venture at a secret history, came out in 1736, but it appeared anonymously. After this for a few years she is silent altogether. When she begins to write again in 1742, with her moral tracts on the conduct of serving maids, wives, and husbands, her *Female Spectator* and her *Parrot* and her quiet domestic novels, it is as an author of a very different type that she comes before the public. She seems to have wished to sever the connection with the author of *Love in Excess* and Eliza of the *Dunciad* for good. The name of "Eliza Haywood" appears no longer on the title page: she calls herself "Mira" or "Euphrosine"—two names first adopted by her in the *Female Spectator*—and, when she has been successful with one book, its title is used as an advertisement for the next. Hence at the end of her life she is simply the "Author of *Betsy Thoughtless*." This anonymity is an evidence that Mrs Haywood did not quite live down the attack on her; it is a tribute to the power of Pope to make or mar the reputations of his weaker

[40] Pope, *Works*, IV, p. 141.

brethren. But it is to her credit that she did not allow herself to be beaten altogether and that, in the changed character of her later years, she was, again, a popular writer.

Pope's attack was the worst blow which M^rs Haywood had to meet in her long life, but it was not the only one. Tradition says that the *Court of Carimania* also brought about her arrest by the officers of the government though there is no trustworthy record of her case as there is of M^rs Manley's. The *Monthly Review* for January, 1750 speaks more confidently of a second arrest—this time for the *Letter from H . . . . . . G . . . . . . g Esq.*, a pamphlet containing injudicious praise of the Pretender, of which she may have been the author. She herself speaks of the difficulties she had to face because she was a woman: "that tide of raillery which all of my sex, unless they are very excellent, indeed, must expect when once they exchange the needle for the quill."[41] No one by whose opinion we should be likely to set much store has a good word for her. That Steele, with his usual good nature, dealt gently with her we might guess at from the dedication to the *Surprise or Constancy Rewarded* in which M^rs Haywood is his "most obliged and most obedient servant." But Swift's opinion that she was a "stupid, infamous scribbling woman"[42] was probably the general one of the great Wits of the reign of Anne and George I. Nor, in spite of her reformed character, does she seem to have commended herself to the patrons of the next age; she was hardly the sort of woman to be admitted to Richardson's small court at Northend, and we have no evidence that she ever came to the notice of Johnson. She was only a novelist after all—and to the novel and romance there still clung a tradition of something inferior and even pernicious. She never appealed to the highest class of readers and her popularity in less cultured circles was only a vogue. No one reads M^rs Haywood today, though one might do worse than read *Betsy Thoughtless* or *Jemmy and Jenny Jessamy*.

In spite of Pope and Swift, however, we cannot afford to despise Eliza Haywood. She had no great gifts, but she had a flair for pleasing the public, and her career, from *Love in Excess* to the tracts on conjugal responsibilities that came out in the year of her

[41] M^rs Haywood, *Fair Captive.* 1721. Dedication.

[42] Swift, *Works.* 1883. (ed. Scott.) Vol. XVII, p. 405. In a letter to M^rs Howard. He adds that he has not seen any of M^rs Haywood's productions so is merely repeating current opinion.

death, is a lesson in adaptability. No one can deny that Mrs Haywood had her wits about her. She was even willing to develop a new personality as the times required it, and the change from the fancy picture of Eliza "in flowers and pearls by Bounteous Kirkall dressed,"[43] in the first collected edition of her works in 1724, to the portrait of the group of respectable dames who represent the editors of the *Female Spectator*—probably only four aspects of the one editor, who was Mrs Haywood—is symbolic. Call her "cast-off dame," "infamous scribbling woman" or what you will, Mrs Haywood's thirty-five years of authorship are something in themselves. When a woman has written seventy or more works, most of them popular, the critics are at length disarmed. When Mrs Haywood died, it was no longer possible to say that women could not write; the woman author had outlived the fabulous-monster period of her existence.

> Read proud usurper, read with conscious shame,
> Pathetic Behn or Manley's greater name
> Forget their sex and own When Haywood writ
> She clos'd the fair Triumvirate of Wit.

When James Sterling wrote these lines in the poem included in the first collected edition of Mrs Haywood's works, he showed an unusual sense of fitness in grouping her with Astraea and Rivella, rather than with Sappho and Anna Von Schurman, after the general uncritical style of eulogists. These three may be taken together as marking one stage in the progress of the woman novelist. All three, without being women of genius or women of high character, managed to achieve fame in their own day as writers. They competed with men, as novelists and playwrights. Mrs Manley in the *Examiner* and Mrs Haywood still more in the *Female Spectator* showed that women could be successful as editors and journalists. Nor did they always blindly follow the men: Mrs Behn was experimenting in *Oroonoko* and Mrs Manley in the *Atlantis*. To earn their livelihood they showed themselves capable of turning a hand to whatever was needed, political pamphleteering, satire of manners, translation, literary criticism. There is a certain similarity in their lives; all three were at some period kept mistresses, and all, in the course of their lives, managed to get themselves into prison. Perhaps their very notoriety was part of their success; in the movement towards the freedom of the woman

[43] *Dunciad*, II, l. 157. (*Works*, IV, p. 282.)

author, they are like the "militants" in the van of the women suffragists who had to call attention to themselves by breaking windows. Had they been less ready to fall in with the manners of an age of brutality and corruption, they might have gone under in the struggle to earn a living; had they been outside the necessity of earning a living, they might never have written at all. We cannot judge them by the moral standards of a later age, nor even by the standards of the ladies of their own time, who sat at home in their country houses and wrote poems and stories for love. Whatever we may think of the "fair triumvirate" or of their works, we have to admit in them the courage, the energy, and versatility which opened up the way for a new type of woman writer.

## CHAPTER II

## THE "LADY" NOVELIST

### 1. From Addison to Richardson

Mrs Haywood's long life stretched over four reigns and almost into a fifth. By the time she died a change had come about in the position of the woman author. She herself, as we have seen, by her sheer persistence, had helped to wear down the critics—but this was not all. More attention was being given to women in general, their minds, their morals, their education. Had Mary Astell's scheme, outlined (in 1697) in the second part of her *Serious Proposal*, been carried, into execution, as it very nearly was, there would have been a women's college in England at the beginning of the eighteenth century—"a retreat for those ladies who, nauseating the pride of the world, might here find a happy recess from the noise and hurry of it."[1] But the Church, in the person of Bishop Burnet, intervened in this unseemly plan and by demonstrating to Princess Anne that it was contrary to the interests of religion, persuaded her to withdraw the generous endowment which was to have built the college. The *Tatler*, of course, had its laugh at Mary Astell,[2] for the earnest woman is one of the immortal jokes of this world, and Steele and Swift and Addison were only taking the attitude of those Victorians who laughed at Miss Buss and Miss Beale. The very fact that Miss Astell got into the *Tatler*, however, showed that her opinions were widely

[1] Ballard, *Memoirs of Learned Ladies in the seventeeth and eighteenth Centuries.* I, p. 307.

[2] *Tatler.* Sept. 1, 1709. (No. 63.)

known, and the earnestness that exposed her to ridicule was enough to make some readers think more seriously of the question of women's education.

That Mary Astell was not purely fantastic in considering the improvement of a woman's mind her "greatest interest," was demonstrated by the presence of a few learned and cultured women among the glittering "ladies of St. James." There was Elizabeth Elstob,[3] most unfeminine of scholars, who edited Saxon homilies and compiled an Anglo-Saxon grammar; there was Mrs Cockburn, the defender of Locke; there was Lady Mary Wortley Montagu, who found time to translate Epictetus in the intervals of a gay life in the world. The "matchless Orinda" had worthy successors in the woman poets of the early eighteenth century—in "Ardelia," Lady Winchilsea,[4] whose exalted rank and retired life could still not preserve her from ill-natured attack; and in "Philomela," Elizabeth Singer, Mrs Rowe, whose piety and poetry brought her the distinction of a long memoir in the *Gentleman's Magazine*.[5] There were, besides, ladies who, like their great Elizabethan predecessors, impressed their contemporaries by themselves rather than by what they wrote: Mrs Catherine Bovey, whom Ballard includes in his memoirs of learned ladies on the ground of "her extraordinary merit, her exemplary life, and the noble use she made of an ample fortune"; and the Lady Elizabeth Hastings, lady bountiful of Ledstone Park in Yorkshire; both of whom have been immortalized by the "divine compliments" of Steele. To get a right perspective of the times we must see all these ladies standing in the background while Mrs Manley and Mrs Haywood fight their way through the crowd in the forefront of the stage.

[3] Elizabeth Elstob (1683-1756) who from the age of fifteen worked with her brother, William Elstob of University College, Oxford, on Anglo-Saxon Grammar and Literature. Her first work, the *Homily on the Birthday of St. Gregory*, was published in 1709. Her *Grammar* was published in 1715, and a proposal, never fully carried out, was made to print an edition, by her, of the Saxon *Homilarium*.

[4] Anne Kingsmill, Lady Winchilsea (1661–1720) a Maid of Honour of the Restoration Court who retired, after her marriage with Colonel Finch, to Eastwell Park and published a volume of poems in 1713. In 1717 she was attacked by Pope and Gay in *Three Hours after Marriage*.

[5] Elizabeth Singer, Mrs Rowe (1674–1737) published in 1696 a volume of Poems under the name of Philomela. A long account of her begins in the *Gentleman's Magazine* for May, 1739.

While women of noble family and gentlewomen throughout the reigns of Anne and George I wrote poetry and works of scholarship, they left the writing of fiction to M$^{rs}$ Manley and her kind. It might be asked why this happened, for story-writing seems a highly suitable employment for the amateur—more suitable, we should think today, than editing Saxon homilies and translating from the Greek. The truth is that the novel was still in disrepute. From Ascham onwards, the educated Englishman seems to have fled from the romance as from the plague, and the tradition persisted into the eighteenth century. The French romance which had delighted Dorothy Osborne in Anne's reign was rapidly becoming a stock joke. It was still read—Lady Mary Wortley Montagu, that "rake in reading," confesses that in her youth she had a great fondness for *Astraea*—but it must have been with a sense of guilt that anyone gave his time to d'Urfé and the Scudérys, in the face of all the criticism which these authors called forth. M$^{rs}$ Manley and M$^{rs}$ Haywood were both consciously trying to get away from the artificiality of the romances and to offer something better to the public in the way of fiction. M$^{rs}$ Manley, especially, in her preface to *Queen Zarah*, shows that she knows very well what is wrong with them and enumerates their weaknesses clearly enough—the prodigious length, the number of extraordinary adventures, the overcrowding of the stage with actors, the sententiousness and the improbability of the characters. Two ideas lie behind her criticism, the first being that the aim of fiction is to please, and the second that this aim can be best attained where the fiction is true to life. But she cannot carry out her ideas, and while her novels gain in realism they lose in their departure from "the unparalleled purity" that made the Scudérys safe reading, at least, for the young lady.

The poor reader then was in a dilemma. If he read romances of the old school, he was filling his head with nonsensical ideas and seeing the world through a flawed glass that would distort the conceptions of life which he might form; if, on the other hand, he turned to M$^{rs}$ Manley and M$^{rs}$ Behn, he was reading a good deal of scandalous and immoral stuff that could not possibly have a good effect on his character. The situation was especially hard on the woman reader. She had not the solace of politics and philosophy, for these were above her head; she was untrained in the classics and could not turn to the past to make up for the deficiencies of her own age; she must not read romance for fear of becoming a Female Quixote with ideas above her household task; most of all she must not read that terrible M[rs] Manley. What should she read? To this question her own age replied unhesitatingly. "Next to the HOLY SCRIPTURES," writes George Hickes, D. D., Dean of Worcester and Chaplain in ordinary to his Majesty,[6] "the young lady should read THE WHOLE DUTY OF MAN; THE LADIES CALLING; and THE GOVERNMENT OF THE TONGUE. After these let her read D[r] Cave's PRIMITIVE CHRISTIANITY to give her an idea of the lives and manners of the ancient Christians; with these she may join his LIVES OF THE APOSTLES and A COMPANION FOR THE FESTIVALS OF THE CHURCH OF ENGLAND by Robert Nelson Esq. She ought not likewise to be unacquainted with A SERIOUS PROPOSAL TO THE LADIES FOR THE ADVANCEMENT OF THEIR TRUEST AND GREATEST INTEREST, in two parts, nor with THE CHRISTIAN RELIGION AS PROFESSED BY A DAUGHTER OF THE CHURCH OF ENGLAND. These two, being written by one of her own sex, may probably serve to make a deeper impression upon her and will be both instructive and delightful." D[r] Hickes, whose reading list, by the way, does not stop here but goes on to suggest another dozen or more works of equal weight, may be suspected of taking a churchman's view of the case, but we find his opinion supported by the men of the world, as represented by the *Spectator*. The *Ladies Library*, which Steele brought out in 1714, contained no more stimulating reading than that which the good Dean of Worcester recommended, being, in fact, a compilation of the *Ladies Calling*, Halifax's *Advice to a Daughter*, *Holy Living*, Tillotson's *Sermons*, and other books of a devotional character, popular at the time. To the Leonoras of the age, such a collection must have seemed a poor exchange for the library containing *Clelia*, *Astraea*, and the "*New Atlantis* with a key to it," but it was an exchange which was offered to them for their benefit by men who wished to see women better read and better educated.

Really the novel had to wait for Richardson before it could be promoted to an honourable place on the library shelves beside

[6] George Hickes, *Instructions for the Education of a Daughter by the author of Telemachus*. 1688. Quoted by Myra Reynolds in the *Learned Lady in England*. p. 296.

the *Whole Duty of Man* and the *Ladies Calling*. But before 1740 there were one or two women of good character who wrote novels and who, though they had nothing like the vogue of M^rs^ Manley or M^rs^ Haywood, deserve our notice from the mere fact that they condescended to the despised craft of novelist. One of these is M^rs^ Penelope Aubin. Of this lady's life we know little or nothing—not even when she was born or died. All we know of her is what we can piece together from her books—that she was a devout Catholic, that she was a friend of M^rs^ Rowe, that "she had no contemptible share of learning surpassing what is usual in the sex."[7] She was the author of several *Histories* and *Novels*, some of them translations from the French, which appeared between the years 1721 and 1729. As she herself announces in the Preface to *Charlotta du Pont*, "my design in writing is to employ my leisure hours to some advantage to myself and others"; she wrote as an amateur and she wrote with a moral purpose. It is evident that she considered her own work as an antidote to the novels of the "fair triumvirate of wit." "My booksellers say my novels sell tolerably well," she tells us.[8] "I had designed to employ my pen on something more serious and learned: but they tell me I shall meet with no encouragement and advised me to write more modishly, that is less like a Christian . . . .but I leave that to the other female authors my contemporaries whose lives and writings have, I fear, too great a resemblance." Her first editor, who gives her a good advertisement in his Preface, echoes this sentiment, pointing out "that those of the sex who have generally wrote on those subjects have been far from preserving the purity of style and manners which is the greatest glory of a fine writer on any subject, but like fallen angels, having lost their own innocence, seem, as one would think by their writings, to make it their study to corrupt the minds of others."[9] "Purity of style and manners" M^rs^ Aubin certainly had to offer the public, but she had not much else. How far she succeeded in her mission of reclaiming the "giddy youth" of the nation by the examples she set before them in her novels, we have no means of judging, for her contemporaries have omitted to leave us their opinions of her. But from one's own impression of the adventures

[7] Penelope Aubin, Collection of *Histories and Novels* (3 volumes) (date lacking). Vol. I. Preface.

[8] *Ibid.*, III. Preface to the Reader, vi.

[9] *Ibid.*, I. Preface.

of her Lucys and Lucindas, one cannot believe that the popularity of the "fallen angels" suffered much from this competition. The booksellers were right, no doubt, when they told her she was not "modish" enough for the age, and the youth she sought to instruct probably regarded her only as another M^rs^ Haywood—with the tang left out. We need not stop over Penelope Aubin except to notice that here was a woman who wrote blameless novels and wrote them, moreover, without the spur of need.

A more remarkable figure is M^rs^ Jane Barker, whose first collection of novels, *The Entertaining Novels of M^rs^ Jane Barker*, was published in 1715, to be followed by a *Patchwork Screen for LADIES; or LOVE and VIRTUE Recommended; in a COLLECTION of instructive NOVELS* in 1723 and by *The Lining of the Patchwork Screen; designed for the farther ENTERTAINMENT of the LADIES* in 1726. She must have been an old woman when these works were published, for she had appeared before the public as the author of certain *Poetical Recreations* as long before as 1688, the year of *Oroonoko*. Her poems had brought her fame, if only a local fame. Through an undergraduate brother, then at Cambridge she had been introduced into the most select group of University wits that then adorned St. John's College. These young gentlemen seemed to have conspired to turn the head of this innocent miss from the country, with their fulsome compliments to her "warbling quill," and, when at length she published her verse, it was to the accompaniment of a most outrageous strain of eulogy from her brother's fellow students.

When in a Comick sweetness you appear
Ben Johnson's humour seems revived there
When lofty Passions thunder from your pen
Me thinks I hear great Shakspear once again.[10]

So writes one of them, a certain C. G., and it is a fair sample of the rest. It is no wonder later in life when the "gobling" of spinsterdom was an established fact and men had proved deceivers, that Jane Barker looked back with bitterness on the time when she was the idol of an elegant, academic coterie, now dispersed for ever, when Fellows and Gentlemen Commoners vied with each other in the gallant game of praising her "incomparable Muse."

It was at this happy period of her life that Miss Barker suffered a disappointment in love, which seems to have soured

[10] Jane Barker, *Poetical Recreations*. Preface.

her for the rest of her days. To mend her broken heart, she took to learning; to Latin Grammar first, then to the more practical studies of medicine and agriculture. Her attitude toward her own higher education is curious. She is quite obviously vain of her knowledge—note the pride with which she speaks of her Latin prescriptions. She welcomes her books also—as a relief from the tormenting thoughts of her false lover. Yet in spite of all this, she is persuaded that studies are unfeminine. She was too well grounded in the tradition that a learned woman is a freak of nature to be comfortable about her learning. Much as she enjoyed the hours spent with her Harvey, she was firmly convinced that these medical books only made her "unfit company for everybody else." "How useless, or rather pernicious, books and learning are to our sex," she bursts forth on one occasion.[11] "They are like oatmeal and charcoal to the depraved appetites of girls, for by their means we relish not the diversions or imbellishments of our sex and station." Then in another mood, she will take out her book and throw up her chin, and say she does not repent of her useless learning. She cannot forbear to make her heroine, Scipiana, learned above the generality of her sex, yet she must needs criticise her through the mouth of the admirable Asiaticus, who forgets for the moment that he is an ancient Roman, and tells her in his best eighteenth century manner, that her books have "spoilt her for marriage." "A singular anomaly" indeed was this lady novelist, who could manage a farm and expound the mysteries of anatomy, yet who envied all the while the featherbrained misses round Wilsthorpe whose knowledge went just far enough to get them husbands.

When Miss Barker forsook poetry, and took to romance, she showed herself fully aware of the prejudice of the age against novels. By her novels, however, she intended to remove this prejudice. In place of the "loose gallantry and libertinism" too often a part of the novels of the day, she sets out to dispense "handfuls of good morality." By the example of her virtuous ancient Romans, she will preach virtue for the age; the nobility of her heroes in adversity will help her readers to distinguish between true worth and a laced coat. If it is love she writes of, it is not love in excess but a sober passion which is the foundation of happy marriages. The *Entertaining Novels* in fact, if they are all their author claimed for them, would have put the *Ladies Calling* out of office.

[11] Jane Barker, *Patchwork Screen.* p. 78.

At the same time the novels are to be entertaining—the author does not forget to make this clear to her public, in the title of her first collection. And was it Jane or was it Curll who saw to it that the word which leapt to the reader's eye on the title of the *Patchwork Screen* should be "Novels" whereas the less alluring word "instructive" should be hidden away in smaller type? Her anxiety to recommend herself to her public is amusing. There is a delightfully naïve preface to the *Entertaining Novels*, in which she disarms criticism before it is offered by stating her own good points to the reader.

"First that the author was certainly in love when she wrote; so 'tis to be hoped that passion is rightly represented. In the next place, 'twas liked because 'twas free from long speeches, and tedious descriptions of towns, places, seiges, battles, horses and their trappings, etc. Nevertheless I have since put in one description (and but one) which is pretty long, and that is of a garden; but it being added since the book was composed, those who love not descriptions, may pass it over unread, without any prejudice to the substantial part of the story."

This passage is of psychological interest to the student of Jane Barker, and at the same time, a comment on the taste of the reading public of her time.

Jane Barker, with the best intentions in the world, set out to vindicate the novel. She hoped, by combining amusement with instruction, to unite grave and gay in her favour. That her novels are above reproachisundoubted; that they were entertaining, even to the age she lived in, is not so certain; and most readers would find the process of getting through *Exilius* a long way round if moral precepts were the only end. In spite of all the author can say for herself, we cannot imagine that either the *Entertaining Novels* or the *Patchwork Screen* seriously threatened the popularity either of M^rs Manley or the *Whole Duty of Man*. Miss Barker is above all else interesting to us as the first "lady" novelist. She was not great enough to establish the respectability of the novel; but she was, nevertheless, a novelist and respectable.

Such was the situation when Richardson began to write. In 1740, after a miserable ten years which produced hardly a novel of any kind, appeared *Pamela: or Virtue Rewarded*, and immediately everthing was changed. "Who could have dreamed," writes

Aaron Hill,[12] "that he should find under the modest guise of a novel all the soul of religion, good breeding, discretion, good nature, wit, fancy, fine thought and morality." Who would have dreamed it, indeed? but the age found all this and more in *Pamela*. One clergyman[13] preached *Pamela* in the pulpit and another[14] compared it with the Bible; Pope, the veteran, prophesied, before he died, that it would "do more good than many volumes of sermons"; when Pamela's virtue was rewarded by the marriage with her Squire, the villagers of Slough set the church bells ringing. If Richardson had had his doubts, before, about introducing his moral lessons to the world in the guise of a novel, the reception of *Pamela* must have removed his fears for ever.

The effect of *Pamela* on the English novel was, of course, enormous, but this is not the place to discuss it. Richardson concerns us here only in so far as he affected the women novelists who came after him. In this connection, two main points emerge. In the first place, by making the novel a means of showing "virtue rewarded," he asserted triumphantly its claim to a high place in the literary hierarchy, according to the ideas of the eighteenth century. In the second place, he brought the novel home to real life. Others had felt vaguely the need for greater realism in the novel, but no one, before Richardson, had managed to get away entirely from the characters and conventions of the glittering world of romance. In writing of Pollys and Pamelas instead of Bellamoras and Philadelphias, of Derbyshire and Bedfordshire instead of Atlantis and Utopia, he set a value on the everyday things of life, which had always been beneath the notice of the writer of romance. In both these ways Richardson opened up infinite possibilities to women. After *Pamela* no woman need be ashamed to have her name connected with the novel: it was no longer frivolous, no longer immoral; it was recommended by Doctors of Divinity and placed in the category of sermons. After *Pamela* too, the scene of the novel was shifted and the new setting was one which was well known to women. If matter for fiction were to be found in the servants' halls and the cedar parlours of country houses, here was a chance for women to write of the things they knew. Dorothy Osborne had appreciated to the full the little

[12] Richardson, *Correspondence*. 1804. (ed. Barbauld.) Vol. I, p. 53.

[13] Dr Slocock of St. Saviour's, Southwark.

[14] The Rev. Mr Smyth Loftus. *Correspondence*. V, p. 178.

humours and pleasures of her quiet, domestic life at Chicksands, but it had never occurred to her to make a story of them. Had she lived in the days after *Pamela* she might, perhaps, have made of her life a tale to be read by more than Sir William Temple.

As much as his books, however, we must take into consideration the influence of Richardson himself in bringing about a change in the position of women. *Pamela* made his fame, *Clarissa* established it, and, after 1742, Richardson was the foremost Man of Letters of his day. The printer of Salisbury Court succeeded the great M^r^ Pope as Dictator to the literary world. One sees at once that a society which would elect Richardson as its president would be far more susceptible to feminine influence than that ruled over by Addison and Steele and, later, by Pope. Addison laughing tolerantly at the fair sex, Steele, their very humble servant, Pope loving and hating by turns, to conclude in the end that "most women have no character at all"—all these gave their best to the society of men. Richardson on the other hand delighted in the companionship of women. Richardson would have been terribly ill at ease if he had strayed by chance into the Kit-Cat Club. Fielding would have been at home there but not Richardson. A water-drinker, a vegetarian, a good apprentice who married his master's daughter, Richardson was without the masculine "vices" which are the virtues of the boon companion. He wanted the power to let himself go which the man must have who is to be popular in men's society. There is something in the conviviality of the Kit-Cat meetings—as there is in the company of the Boar's Head Tavern in Eastcheap, which women do not quite appreciate—and in this, Richardson was more a woman than a man. To change the pronoun in that most expressive line which Chaucer wrote of Canace

> *He* was ful mesurable as wommen be.[15]

One thinks of Richardson, as he is shown in Miss Highmore's picture, sitting in the grotto at North End and reading his own books aloud to a select group of friends. And always in that group we find a goodly proportion of women.

Richardson, doubtless, chose the company of women partly because it gave him a greater feeling of security. Where he was unquestionably the greatest of his company, he was safe from

[15] Chaucer, *Squiere's Tale.* l. 362.

ridicule, and he was always a little afraid of the laughter of men like Fielding. "Poor Fielding," he says, laying down *Amelia* half read—but in his heart he was not convinced of his superiority over "poor Fielding." He knew that Fielding had the unhappy gift of being able to put him out of countenance. But among women his superiority was unquestioned. It is a beautiful picture of hero worship—Richardson in his "flower-garden" of ladies. We see him gravely discussing the character of Sir Charles Grandison with Miss Mulso, gently teasing Miss Highmore about her Mr Duncombe, arguing, with half his strength, on the education of women with Lady Bradshaigh. How delighted they are that the great man should give up his time to them! Sarah Fielding is like a schoolgirl over a letter from Mr Richardson. "You cannot imagine the pleasure Miss Collier and I enjoyed at the receipt of your kind epistles," she writes to him.[16] "We were at dinner with a hic, haec, hoc man who said, 'Well, I do wonder Mr Richardson will be troubled with such silly women,' on which we thought to ourselves (though we did not care to say it), if Mr Richardson will bear us and not think us impertinent in pursuing the pleasure of his correspondence, we don't care in how many languages you fancy you despise us." Of course, Mr Richardson would bear them so long as they flattered him to the top of his bent. He was as delighted as they when Susan Highmore consulted him about the state of her heart, because he was so "indulgent to lover's foibles"[17]—or when Hester Mulso, his "dear Hecky," took her troubles to him as her "mental Aesculapius"[18]—or when Lady Bradshaigh exclaims in admiration, "Oh! sir, you ought to have been a bishop!"[19] "I cannot forbear priding myself on my girls," he says complacently.[20] One hopes that he was grateful, too, to his "girls", for they were an army enlisted against all his critics.

This companionship, however, meant a good deal to the women who were admitted to it. It was not merely that they derived a certain intellectual stimulus from their contact with a great writer; it was, also, that they felt the honour conferred upon their sex and

[16] Richardson, *Correspondence.* II, p. 59.

[17] *Ibid.*, II, p. 221.

[18] *Ibid.*, III, p. 282.

[19] *Ibid.* (Quoted by Miss C. L. Thomson from Bradshaigh MSS. *Samuel Richardson.* p. 55.)

[20] *Ibid.*, III, p. 287.

held their heads the higher for it. There is no doubt that Richardson was considered by his age as the champion of the female sex. It was not merely that a needy authoress, like Letitia Pilkington, could turn to him for money and a "character." Swift was the patron of women, as far as that goes, and Swift was no feminist. Richardson himself is conscious of occupying a special position with regard to women. To Lady Bradshaigh he calls himself "an advocate of your sex"; Margaret Collier, friend of the Fieldings and companion of Henry Fielding on his voyage to Lisbon writes to Richardson as "the *only* candid man . . . . with regard to women's understandings, and indeed their only champion and protector . . . . in your writings."[21] He is, indeed, an upholder of women's education. In long debate on the subject which took place between them,[22] it is Lady Bradshaigh and not Richardson who takes the reactionary line. All his heroines are women of some education. Clarissa, though she contrives to waste a vast amount of time in her eighteen-hour day, adds to her mastery of music, drawing, and needlework, a knowledge of French, Latin, Italian, and "the four principal rules of arithmetic";[23] Harriet Byron was taught French and Italian by her Grandfather Shirley " a man of universal learning"; even Pamela had to make up for lost time and set out after marriage to acquire French and Latin. A woman anxious to learn, says Richardson, should never be kept back. The oft repeated argument that it might be inconvenient for a woman to know more than her husband, he treats as it should be treated. "If the sex is to be beautiful," he writes to Lady Bradshaigh,[24] "with a view to make the individuals of it inferior in knowledge to the husbands they might happen to have, not knowing who those husbands are or what, or whether sensible or foolish, learned or illiterate, it would be best to keep them from writing and reading and even from the knowledge of the common idioms of speech." Richardson is not a fiery advocate of women's education. He detests the woman scholar who makes a parade of learning and one feels that he would not have cared for the society of women who knew as much as he. "Dear Lady," he says to Lady Bradshaigh, "discourage not the

[21] *Ibid.*, I, p. 77.

[22] For this debate see *Correspondence.* VI where it is carried on through several letters.

[23] Richardson., *Works.* (ed. Leslie Stephen.) Vol. VIII, pp. 458–480.

[24] Richardson, *Correspondence.* VI, p. 58.

sweet souls from acquiring any learning that may keep them employed and out of mischief." But he does try to break down the idea that learning is the prerogative of the male sex. If he would agree with Sir Charles that woman's intellect is "*softer*"—a euphemism for "inferior"—he still believed that many women were superior in mind to many men. If none of his heroines is equal to Sir Charles in his eyes, he still shows Harriet getting the best of it in debate with an Oxford scholar, and even the unlettered Pamela putting to shame the ridiculous M^r^ H . . . . . .

What Richardson is pleading more effectually in the characters of his heroines is the right of women to be judged by the same ethical standards as men—or, if he does not go quite so far as that, at least he is questioning the right of men to have a moral law unto themselves. Pamela's morality is not a very admirable one, but at least she is the superior of the man she married. The conception of morality in *Clarissa* is something far greater—greater, indeed, than one would have believed possible in a man who thought that Pamela's marriage was virtue rewarded. Both books in their different ways are, however, a protest against certain moral ideas that were current at the time—that a reformed rake makes the best husband; that honour is an affair between man and man, and women are fair game for tricks and deceptions; that a man's imperfections are no plea for a woman's. Richardson is raising a problem here which has never been settled to this day—a problem which Hardy showed in the clearest light in the scene in the farmhouse after Tess's marriage with Angel Clare. And, by his insistence on women's virtue, by the superiority of character which he gives to his heroines he is helping to raise the general opinion of women.

I have dwelt at length on Richardson's attitude to women because I think it is almost impossible to make too much of it. He was patronizing, he was superior, and he was vain. But after all he was a man with a European reputation, one whose works were translated into several languages and whom distinguished persons came from abroad to see as the creator of the "divine Clarissa." That Miss Mulso,[25] the "sweet linnet," should be able to go

[25] Hester Mulso (1727–1801) has several connections with literary people. She became acquainted with Richardson soon after the publication of *Clarissa*. Her brother Thomas married Miss Prescott, another of Richardson's "girls". She herself married in 1760 John Chapone, son of Sarah Chapone, the friend of M^r^

to such a man with her indifferent poems; that Miss Talbot[26] should be consulted by him with regard to the language of *Sir Charles Grandison*, that Miss Highmore[27] should discuss with him the character of Harriet as it unfolds, that Mrs Klopstock[28] found in him a sympathetic friend to whom she could write "pretty letters" about her wonderful husband—all these things mark a very great change in the relations of women with the great men of letters. He was, as Mrs Barbauld puts it, "A friend to mental improvement in women, though under all those restrictions which modesty and decorum have imposed upon the sex." The restrictions are still there; but we have, nevertheless, travelled a long way from the literary society of Mr Spectator.

## 2. SARAH FIELDING, 1710–1768

"Your *Clarissa* is, I find, the virgin mother of several pieces," wrote Dr Young to Richardson in 1749.[29] Even before that date, indeed, we see the influence of Richardson at work on other novelists. In 1744 appeared a novel by one of the women of his own intimate circle, *The Adventures of David Simple, containing an Account of his Travels through the Cities of London and Westminster in the Search of a Real Friend. By a Lady.* This Lady was Sarah Fielding.

We know very little of Sarah Fielding's life. She was born at East Stower in Dorsetshire in 1710, three years after her brother Henry, and was probably educated at home in the "Reading, Writing, Working and all the proper forms of Behaviour," which, according to her *Little Female Academy*, constituted the essentials

---

Delaney, and her best known work, the *Letters on the Improvement of the Mind* (1773) belongs to the period after her marriage. She was also an occasional contributor to the *Rambler*, *Adventurer*, and *Gentleman's Magazine*.

[26] Catherine Talbot (1721–1770) was the friend and correspondent of Elizabeth Carter, who collected and published the *Works of Catherine Talbot* in 1770. The reference to the revision of *Sir Charles Grandison* is in Miss Carter's *Correspondence* (1809). II, p. 142.

[27] Susanna Highmore (1730–1812) was the daughter of Joseph Highmore, the artist, and married in 1763 John Duncombe, a friend of Richardson's and author of the *Feminead*, in which Miss Highmore is represented in the character of Eugenia.

[28] Mrs Klopstock was the wife of the German poet Klopstock, author of the *Messiah*, which she offered to translate for Richardson's benefit. She died in 1758. For her letters see *Correspondence*. III, pp. 140–158.

[29] Richardson, *Correspondence*. I, p. cxliii.

of the education of the young gentlewoman of the day. That her own education did not stop there, we know from her works. *David Simple* abounds in quotations and references from English and French literature—sometimes a little ostentatiously dragged in; and her translation of the *Memorabilia* of Xenophon is a testimony to her Greek scholarship in the days when Greek was very rarely a female accomplishment. Where she lived while her brother was squandering his patrimony and writing farces for a living in London is uncertain, but at one period she was in Salisbury, making the acquaintance of Jane and Margaret Collier, with whom she afterwards lived; and, about 1741, we find her in London, becoming initiated into the circle of Richardson. For ten years after the publication of *David Simple* she seems to have been living with her brother and the Colliers in London, dependent on his charity and her own writing. During this time she must have been often at North End, and, in 1748,[30] she was eagerly requesting the privilege of being employed as the amanuensis of the creator of the "divine Clarissa," the hem of whose garment, she protests, she is not worthy to touch. In 1754 she was at Bath, while her brother and Margaret Collier made the voyage to Lisbon, and to Bath she retired in the last years of her life, and died there in 1768. After *David Simple* she wrote no more novels though she published a sequel to it in 1747. Later she collaborated with Jane Collier in the *Cry*, (1754) which they called a "dramatic fable" and wrote moral stories for children in her *Little Female Academy* (1749). The rest of her works include the *Lives of Cleopatra and Octavia* (1757), *The History of Ophelia* (1758), and the *Memorabilia* (1762).

The words "By a Lady," on the title-page of *David Simple* are in the nature of a challenge. But the author still feels she must apologize for the fact of her authorship.

"The following moral romance," she says in her Preface to the first edition, "is the work of a woman and her first Essay, which, to the good-natured and candid reader, it will be hoped, is a sufficient apology for the many inaccuracies he will find in the style and other faults of the composition. Perhaps the best excuse that can be made for a woman's venturing to write at all, is that which really produced this book; Distress in her Circumstances, which she could not so well remove by any other means in her power."

[30] Richardson, *Correspondence.* I, p. 61.

This preface introduces to the public a new class of author—the needy gentlewoman. The world, however, was not yet used to the idea that a woman was capable of writing anything of the type of *David Simple*. Somehow the name of "Fielding" leaked out and immediately the book was put down to Henry's credit. In the second edition of the novel, we find a Preface "by the Author of *Tom Jones*," in which he denies that he is also the author of *David Simple*—not, as he points out, because he is ashamed of it, but "to do justice to the real and sole author." It is the old story—the Duchess of Newcastle's works were ascribed to the Duke, Aphra Behn's plays were written by Ravenscroft, and now Sarah Fielding's novel was given to her brother.

That Henry Fielding should have been suspected of having written *David Simple* is a reflection of the sheer perversity and want of critical judgment of the public who accused him. One may take his word for it that he contributed to his sister's novel nothing more than a few hints and suggestions. Some touches of satire in *David Simple*—the portraits of characters in the stagecoach or of the circle of female critics—show that Miss Fielding looked on life at times from the same angle as her brother. But the whole tone of the book, the character of David, the death of Daniel, the sentimental episodes, and the ubiquitous moral suggest that Richardson rather than Fielding was its inspiration. Henry Fielding speaks warmly and affectionately in praise of his sister in the Preface; he even goes so far as to say that her book contains some touches which "might have done honour to the pencil of the immortal Shakespeare himself." But we feel that it was to Richardson that Sarah Fielding would turn for advice and encouragement. Richardson we can imagine talking over with her the development of her characters with all necessary seriousness, but can we imagine Fielding in the same position? Fielding on the voyage to Lisbon, tired out by the society of women, is sighing for a "conversible *man*"[31] to talk to "with as much of the qualifications of learning, sense and good-humour as ye can find, who will drink a moderate glass in an evening or will at least sit up till one with me when I do." Kind and generous as he was to her, Fielding would not seek the society of his sister while he could find a "conversible man." One may envy Sarah Fielding her opportunities, in the society of a literary brother, but one is forced to the conclusion, nevertheless,

[31] Cross, *History of Henry Fielding*. III, p. 56.

that she got more out of the society of the middle-class M^r Richardson, whom Fielding despised and who tried to despise Fielding in his turn. What she thought of her brother we do not know, but she seems to have listened calmly to Richardson's criticism of him and probably, under the influence of such criticism, to have come to be a little ashamed of his moral standards, which were undoubtedly not those of Sir Charles Grandison.

In that she was a woman of learning and an advocate of women's education, also, Miss Fielding could expect more sympathy from Richardson than from her brother. Henry Fielding lets us see from his novels what he thought of the learned lady as a type. M^rs Western is contrasted unfavourably with his ideal maid, Sophia, and M^rs Bennet with his ideal wife, Amelia. Underlying his portraits of learned women is the assumption that their pursuit of knowledge is only an unwilling alternative to married life. In M^rs Western, critic, politician, and woman of the world, the prototype, moreover, of the woman suffragist, Fielding is drawing a picture of the spinster, disappointed in her hopes of love. Her political pamphlets and Gazettes are her substitute for a husband; her "advanced" views on the emancipation of women are born of the restlessness which is apt to overtake the woman who is not rooted in a domestic life of her own. A happy wife like Amelia does not care whether she is emancipated or not. Even the learning of Fielding's learned women is not sound. M^rs Western quotes from Milton what Milton never wrote, and M^rs Bennet, in *Amelia*, for all her boasted knowledge of the classics is easily caught out by D^r Harrison. Fielding has more sympathy for old Squire Western in his "more than Gothic ignorance" than for women such as these. We see his own point of view expressed in D^r Harrison's debates with M^rs Bennet on the matter of her classical education—she arguing with all earnestness, he gently playing with her. "If you are one of those who imagine women incapable of learning," says she defiantly, "I shall not be offended at it. I know the common opinion . . . ."[32]

"If I were to profess such an opinion, madam," said the doctor, "Madam Dacier and yourself would bear testimony against me." "Madame Dacier and yourself"—there speaks the typical "male man" of the eighteenth century, terminating the argument with a compliment. It is the same attitude as Fontenelle's to his

[32] Fielding, *Works*. 1902. 12 volumes. (ed. Saintsbury.) *Amelia*, III, p. 65.

Marchioness, Addison's to the family of Lady Lizard. Mudford, in his prefaces to the series of British Novelists which he published in 1811, conjectures that Fielding's dislike of the learned woman sprung from his having observed the "pernicious consequences" of learning in his sister, Sarah. I believe it was due to something more fundamental than this; and that indeed, if anything softened his feeling toward the learned lady, it was his fondness for his scholar sister. But the fact remains that Sarah was not the type of woman to appeal to her brother, who preferred Charlotte Craddock, the model of Sophia Western and Amelia. The ties of blood were stronger in uniting the Fieldings than any ties formed through mutual sympathies and interests.

In the character of Cynthia in *David Simple* Sarah Fielding answers the kind of criticism which is embodied in the character of M^rs^ Western. Cynthia, who takes her pleasure in books, is told that reading will never get her a husband. Her reply is that the husband who would think her education a disadvantage is not worth having. "I could not help reflecting on the folly of those women," she says,[33] "who prostitute themselves (for I shall always call it prostitution, for a woman who has sense and has been tolerably educated, to marry a clown and a fool) and give up that enjoyment, which every one who has taste enough to know how to employ their time, can procure for themselves, though they should be obliged to live ever so retired, only to know they have married a man with an estate." One wonders what Fielding thought of this. Probably he did not believe in the woman who preferred retirement and her own devices to a husband and an estate. But where she feels strongly, Sarah is not afraid of conventional opinion. She returns to the subject in the *Familiar Letters between the Principal Characters in David Simple*, when Cynthia in a Bath drawing-room, finds herself forced into defending the woman author against the attacks of the empty-headed Elmira and the vapid Corydon. Their contentions are the old ones we have heard so often; that it is not proper for a woman to write; that no woman could write even if she would. When the keen-witted Cynthia corners them, by superior logic, they content themselves with the conclusion that "some women might be capable of writing, if they had not judgment enough to know it was not proper

[33] Sarah Fielding, *David Simple*. (ed. Baker. *Half Forgotten Books* Series.) p. 115.

for them."[34] For creatures such as these, and the society that supported them, Cynthia—and Sarah herself—can find no words to express her contempt.

The novel, for Sarah Fielding, was a means of speaking her mind on the follies of the age and of attacking any conventional ideas which seemed to her in need of revision. It was also a means of inculcating a Christian moral. Other woman writers had pretended to a moral purpose; even Mrs Manley had drawn morals of a highly practical type from her scandalous stories, as, for instance, "that no woman ought to introduce another to the man by whom she is beloved."[35] But there is a certain solidity in *David Simple* that is lacking in any of the earlier romances. Today, Sarah Fielding is worth reading for the shrewdness of her comments on the age she lived in. In her own times, when the follies she satirized were living abuses, and her ideas on marriage and education came home to her readers, she must have been regarded as a writer of no little weight. "What a knowledge of the human heart! Well might a critical judge of writing, say, as he did to me that your late brother's knowledge of it was not (fine writer as he was) comparable to yours. His was but as the knowledge of the outside of a clock-work machine, while yours was that of all the finer springs and movements of the inside."[36] This glowing praise of the new woman novelist was written by Richardson and the "critical judge of writing" he refers to is no other than Johnson.

## 3. CHARLOTTE LENNOX 1720–1804

Sarah Fielding was the only one of Richardson's "girls" who became a well-known novelist. Most of the women of his circle, it is true, were inspired to write something: Miss Mulso and Miss Highmore were both minor poets; Catherine Talbot was the author of *Reflections on the Seven Days of the Week*, and other moral works. Urania Hill, eldest of the three daughters of Aaron Hill, whom Richardson called his "dear family Clarissas," did, indeed, attempt a novel, the *Almira* which Richardson criticized on the grounds of its indelicacy; but it has gone the way of other forgotten books, and *David Simple* remains the one novel of any note produced by a woman in direct contact with the master. Richardson's influence,

[34] *Familiar Letters.* p. 94.
[35] Mrs Manley, *New Atlantis.* I.
[36] Richardson, *Correspondence.* I, p. 104.

however, was not confined to his immediate circle; we have seen already how it could affect even a hardened *romancière* like Mrs Haywood, whose *Betsy Thoughtless* and *Jemmy and Jenny Jessamy* belong to Dr Young's category of the offspring of Clarissa. Contemporary with Sarah Fielding was another poor gentlewoman who wrote novels taking their direction from those of Richardson. This was Mrs Charlotte Lennox.

If *The Life of Harriot Stuart Written by Herself* is a true account of the early life of Charlotte Lennox—Charlotte Rumsey, as she was in those days—we may believe that she had adventures enough to supply her with material for half a hundred novels. We cannot, however, accept the whole of it as autobiography. It is true that she went out to America at an early age, for her father, Colonel James Rumsey (or Ramsey) was Lieutenant Governor of New York. In these years she doubtless laid in the impressions of Albany and the surrounding country and of the customs of the Indians and the Dutch settlers which she turned to good account, later in life, in *Euphemia*, but which are crowded out of the *Life of Harriot Stuart* by the hurry of the events. It is true, also, that she returned to England to the supposed guardianship of an aunt, whom she found, on her arrival, to have gone mad and to have been removed to some retreat in Essex, leaving her niece penniless and unprotected. But the shipwrecks and the kidnappings we cannot accept as facts. Colonel Rumsey was not the man to let his daughter wander about the world, without protection, in the face of all imaginable dangers by land and sea—pirates, Indians, and unscrupulous lovers.

How much Miss Rumsey wished to identify herself with the character of Harriot is again a question. Perhaps we may credit her with something of the untamed lively disposition of her heroine, from the independent spirit she showed in later years; and if we are unwilling to believe that she indulged in affairs of the heart at the rate and the intensity at which Harriot indulged in them, we may well believe that the author of the *Female Quixote* was a romantic girl, enjoying in imagination the adventures which Harriot enjoys in the reality of her book. Two of Harriot's talents were possessed by her creator: her dramatic power that brought her applause for her rendering of Monimia in Otway's *Orphan* and the gift of writing verse, which was her consolation in the unpropitious moments of her love affairs. Miss Rumsey tried her own capacities in both these directions when, on finding herself stranded in London, she set out to support herself as an actress and wrote the poems which she published in 1747. One poem of Harriot's throws some light on the manner of her author's education and amusements. "Let us spend our time," she says to "Delia," a girl friend,

> Repeating Pope's harmonious lays
> Now Homer's awful leaves turn o'er.
> Or graver history explore
> Or study Plato's sacred page,
> Uncommon to our sex and age.[37]

We have, elsewhere, indications that M^rs^ Lennox was no adherent of the education which was common to her sex and age. In *Euphemia* she gives a contemptuous account of the education of M^rs^ Bellenden, the woman of the world, a type with whom she was not in sympathy.

"She can carry on the small talk of a tea table in French," she says, "draws prettily; and is allowed to shade her flowers in embroidery extremely well; but her reading has been wholly confined to her Psalter and Bible, a few devotional tracts and some sermons . . . . she has a great contempt for book-learning in women."[38] M^rs^ Lennox's own knowledge of French went beyond tea table small talk and her reading was wide enough to deserve the formidable appellation of "book-learning."

If, indeed, there is some truth in *Harriot Stuart*, there is more fiction, and purely fictitious is the account of what happened after her return to England and her marriage with the "dangerously lovely" Dumont. What did actually happen, in the period before her marriage with Henry Lennox, in 1748, is not quite clear, except that she was known as "a poetess and a deplorable actress," in Horace Walpole's opinion at least,[39] and that at some time she made the acquaintance of Johnson—M^r^ Johnson, as he was in those days. It was Johnson who on the publication of *Harriot Stuart* in 1751 gave a dinner in honour of the author and Johnson who stood as godfather to the books that followed. In 1752 Charlotte Lennox again turned the experiences of her youth to account in the *Female Quixote* in which she satirizes, from a deep and de-

[37] Charlotte Lennox, *Life of Harriot Stuart*. 1751. II, p. 199.
[38] Charlotte Lennox, *Euphemia*. 1790. I, p. 189.
[39] Horace Walpole, *Letters*. 1903. (ed. M^rs^ Paget Toynbee.) II, p. 337.

tailed knowledge of them, the romances that she had read in her girlhood. This work won the praise of Fielding and of Richardson, and had the distinction of a Dedication written by Johnson and a review by him in the *Gentleman's Magazine*, in the days when Sylvanus Urban gave up very little of his space to book reviews. Lady Mary Wortley Montagu was entertained by it in Italy;[40] and Miss Catherine Talbot, who read everything, speaks of it as "highly diverting and much in fashion."[41] Mrs Lennox now was a famous author. *Henrietta* in 1758 added to her fame as a novelist, and by this time she had also started a reputation for scholarship by her *Shakspere Illustrated* in 1754, and her French translations of the *Memoirs* of Sully, of the Countess of Berci, and of Madame de Maintenon. In 1759 she was chosen as one of the editors of *Brumoy's Greek Theatre*, Johnson being one of her co-editors, and this honour to the sex is commented on by the anonymous editor of Mrs Centlivre's *Works* in 1761, with much satisfaction. "This convinces me," she says,[42] "that not only that barbarious Custom of denying Women to have Souls begins to be rejected as foolish and absurd, but also that foolish Assertion that Female Minds are not capable of producing literary Works, equal even to those of Pope, now loses Ground."

The fame of her writings, however, was not enough to keep Mrs Lennox from distress, for, from the *Proposal* issued by Johnson in 1775 to print her works by subscription we find that what she had received from her works was not enough to keep her, now a widow, and her children. "She hopes," says Johnson,[43] "that she shall not be considered as too indulgent to vanity or too studious of interest, if from that labour which has hitherto been chiefly gainful to others, she endeavours to obtain at last, some profit for herself and her children." But Dr Johnson's *Proposal* came to nothing, and Mrs Lennox was left to find other means of supporting herself. To this end she wrote *Euphemia*, in 1790, but this was her last attempt as a novelist. She survived the period of her popularity and to the readers of the end of the eighteenth century she was no doubt a relic of mid-century, an author grown out of date.

[40] Lady Mary Wortley Montagu, *Letters*. (Everyman.) p. 457.

[41] Elizabeth Carter, *Correspondence*. 1809. II, p. 69.

[42] Mrs Centlivre, *Works*. 1761. Preface "To the World." (Quoted by Myra Reynolds in *Learned Lady in England*. p. 135.)

[43] Boswell, *Life of Johnson*. 1904. (ed. G. B. Hill.) II, p. 331.

The career of Charlotte Lennox illustrates at once the acceptance of the woman author by the world and the precariousness of her position. Her calling was now a respectable one, but it did not carry with it independence. After the death of her husband, M$^{rs}$ Lennox could hardly support herself in spite of hard work and a gift for pleasing the public. Writing, however, is always a precarious living; only, nowadays, owing to the larger reading public, the market value of the popular book has changed. The *Female Quixote* was a "best seller" of its own day, and it could not keep its author; but we have to remember the struggle which even Johnson had to win his independence. If we look at Charlotte Lennox in the period of her fame, however, we see what a long way we have travelled from the time of Aphra Behn. M$^{rs}$ Lennox's career challenges comparison with M$^{rs}$ Behn's from a certain similarity in their upbringing. Both spent their early lives abroad, from the fact that their fathers occupied positions in colonial administration; both were stranded in London when young and turned to writing and to the theatres to support themselves. But while M$^{rs}$ Behn could not win fame without infamy, M$^{rs}$ Lennox had the sincere praise of some of the greatest men of her day.[44] Fielding refers to her as the "inimitable . . . . author of the *Female Quixote*,"[45] Richardson said of her that she had genius, Goldsmith wrote an epilogue for her comedy, *The Sister*, produced in 1769, Sir Joshua Reynolds painted her portrait, and most of all, she was admired by Johnson. There is nothing of condescension or of gallantry, either, in the admiration of Johnson. Even in his later days when he knew many famous women, he recurs again to the name of M$^{rs}$ Lennox. "I dined yesterday at M$^{rs}$ Garrick's," he said in 1784, "with Miss Carter, Miss H. More and Miss Burney. Three such women are not to be found. I know not where I could find a fourth except M$^{rs}$ Lennox, who is superior to them all"[46]—a comparison by the way which seems to have aroused jealousy in Miss Burney, for she finds it necessary to explain it away by saying that Boswell often recorded chance remarks which did not represent Johnson's considered opinions.

The lives of Sarah Fielding and Charlotte Lennox both illustrate the difference in the woman novelist's position, once she

[44] Fielding, *Works*. (ed. Saintsbury.) *Voyage to Lisbon*. p. 165.

[45] Richardson, *Correspondence*. VI, p. 243.

[46] Boswell, *Life of Johnson*. (ed. G. B. Hill.) IV, p. 317.

was backed by the approval of the great men of the age. While Authority, in the *Spectator* or the *Dunciad*, persisted in treating the woman writer as a joke, or worse, the fact that she wrote readable books could do little to mend her position. But as soon as her works were sponsored by Richardson or Johnson her status became changed. The triumph of the "female wit" is well depicted in that scene described by Sir John Hawkins,[47] of the banquet held in honour of the author of *Harriot Stuart*, with its rites and ceremonies, its invocations to the Muses, its "magnificent hot apple pie stuck with bay-leaves;" when Johnson himself, his face "shining with meridian splendour," set the crown of laurel on the head of Charlotte Lennox.

# CHAPTER III

## THE PERIOD OF THE BLUESTOCKINGS

### 1. THE WOMEN OF D^R^ JOHNSON'S CIRCLE

The removal of the literary court from Will's and Button's to North End, Hammersmith, meant, as we have seen, a great change in the position of the woman writer. Literature was no longer the affair of an aristocratic club. The club lived on, indeed, as a resort of the "wits", but the gentlemen who met at White's—Horace Walpole and George Selwyn and the rest, self-confessed Dilettanti—were not the representatives of their age that the "old wits" were in the Kit-Cat days. Nor was Richardson's circle entirely representative, though he was the most widely read and talked-of author of the day, for it excluded too much. On the one hand, Richardson was not accepted by the world of fashion. Even the gracious M^rs^ Delany, much as she admired *Clarissa*, could not quite forget that its author was only a printer; and Fielding and Lady Mary Wortley Montagu laughed openly at his attempts to depict the high society of whose manners he was ignorant. One suspects that Richardson, who was as great a snob as anybody, could not forgive Fielding his advantage over him in birth. On the other hand, Richardson, cut off from "high life," cut himself off from the low. Like the Fellow in *She Stoops to Conquer* he "could not bear anything low." He lacked Fielding's Shakespearian sympathy for "mortal men" and sinners. Lowest of all fellows,

[47] Hawkins, *Life of Johnson*. 1787. p. 286.

indeed, in his eyes, was Tom Jones. Women and clergymen, for the most part, make up the tale of Richardson's friends, and one can see why. For women are less susceptible to caste distinctions than men, and clergymen are outside them; and women by their temperament, clergymen by their calling, are both in sympathy with the "mesurable" morality of Richardson. Of the literary men who were his friends—Aaron Hill, Colley Cibber, Thomas Edwards—all are minor characters in the eighteenth century scene. If we could conceive of a group in which Richardson, Fielding, and Horace Walpole fraternized, we might have the typical literary society of the seventeen-fifties—but imagination boggles at it.

It is not until we come to Johnson—to those later years when he was D^r Johnson and had won the leisure to sit down and talk—that we find a personality great enough to unite elements as various as these and to gather round him a circle as representative of the spirit of the age as Addison's "Little Senate" was of a very different one. The admittance of women to Johnson's society took them into a greater world than Richardson's. At Northend you had Richardson, to be sure; talks with Richardson, advice from Richardson, letters from Richardson; but if you knew Johnson you might also know Burke and Gibbon, Goldsmith and Sheridan, David Garrick and Sir Joshua Reynolds. Fanny Burney's *Diary*, in the days before Johnson died, is dazzling by the brilliance of the names that fill its pages. It would have been a surprising event, indeed, if Mary Astell and Elizabeth Elstob and Lady Winchilsea could have sat down to tea with Addison and Steele and Swift, or with Pope and Gay and Arbuthnot for an amicable discussion on literary matters; it is a picture which, if his bent were not exclusively toward the mediaeval, M^r George Morrow might have added to his "Scenes at which we have never assisted" in *Punch*. Yet half a century later this had become the natural thing. No one exclaimed when Johnson and Garrick sat down with Hannah More and Elizabeth Carter; and Fanny Burney is not overlooked in the company of Sheridan and Sir Joshua or even of Burke and Gibbon. Johnson himself is conscious of the progress made since Addison's day when "in the female world, any acquaintance with books was distinguished only to be censured."[1] He does not give Richardson credit for much disinterestedness, either, in the services which he rendered to the sex; he surrounded himself by

[1] Boswell, *Life of Johnson*. 1904. (ed. G. B. Hill.) VII, p. 107.

women, according to Johnson, because they "listened to him implicitly and did not venture to contradict his opinions."[2] The circle which Johnson drew round him was not composed entirely of men or of women. It made possible the free intercourse of both sexes, and, far more than anything before it, it established their equality.

We have come to associate the women that were famous in the latter half of the eighteenth century with Johnson because Johnson was the magnet which attracted all the best and most brilliant minds of the age. All of them at some time or other sought Johnson's society, but that does not mean that they were in any way dependent on their association with him. Miss Highmore, Miss Westcombe, Miss Prescott we might never have heard of but for Richardson; but Miss Carter and M^rs^ Montagu were mature women of established reputation when they met Johnson, and M^rs^ Delany, M^rs^ Cholmondeley, M^rs^ Boscowen were women of the world of fashion who had no need of patronage. Johnson had his hero worshippers, indeed—neither Fanny Burney nor Hannah More can be acquitted on that score—but the atmosphere in his society is very different from that of the grotto at North End. In point of time we cannot draw a rigid line to divide the women of Richardson's circle from those of Johnson's. M^rs^ Chapone in her middle life was one of the Bluestockings, as Hester Mulso was one of the most intimate of Richardson's friends; Miss Carter touches both groups, though she was never the undiscriminating admirer of Richardson that her friend Miss Talbot was; even M^rs^ Delany was one of Richardson's correspondents. The original Bluestocking assemblies were already being held at M^rs^ Vesey's while Richardson was writing *Sir Charles Grandison*. It is rather that one is conscious of a change in emphasis as one passes from the seventeen-fifties to the seventeen-seventies. When the change took place we cannot say, but there is a change in the position of the woman writer between the time of Sarah Fielding and of Fanny Burney. When *David Simple* was written, it was the woman author's greatest privilege to be introduced to the author of *Clarissa*. When *Evelina* appeared, women were holding courts of their own, and Fanny Burney could write in her diary, "Now that I am invited to M^rs^ Montagu's, I think the measure of my glory is

[2] *Ibid.*, V, pp. 395–6.

full."[3] This she wrote after she had already had the honour of becoming acquainted with D^r Johnson.

Much has been written on Bluestocking society, and it is outside the scope of this study to go into detail on the subject. The women whom Johnson knew in his latter days include scholars, critics, poets, writers on practical morality and social conditions, but not novelists. Fanny Burney occupies a unique position in the circle, and she belongs to a younger generation. But we cannot understand her position without knowing something of her background and, on her account, at least, we must glance at the brilliant group of women who were leaders in the society in which she moved. They have little to do with the history of the novel, but they are all important in the history of Feminism.

Though it was the flighty, elegant M^rs Vesey at whose salons were worn the original blue stockings which first gave the name to the members of her circle, it is Elizabeth Montagu[4] whom we must regard as the Bluestocking *par excellence*, the "Queen of the Blues," as Johnson called her. The work which made her name, the *Essay on the Writings and Genius of Shakespeare*, is not re-

[3] Madame d'Arblay, *Diary*. 1891. (ed. Charlotte Barrett.) I, p. 74.

[4] The following are the principal dates connected with the women mentioned in this section:

Elizabeth Robinson, M^rs Montagu (1720–1800). She contributed three dialogues to Lyttleton's *Dialogues of the Dead* in 1760 and published her *Essay on the Writings and Genius of Shakespeare* in 1769. In 1742 she married Edward Montagu, M.P., who left her a widow in 1775.

Elizabeth Carter (1717–1806). Her *Poems* were published in 1738 and her translation of *Epictetus* in 1757.

Elizabeth Vesey (M^rs Handcocke, M^rs Vesey) (1715–1791). She married for her second husband Agmondesham Vesey, M.P., a member of Johnson's "Club." Both she and her husband were Irish by birth. After her husband's death in 1785, her intellect was permanently weakened.

Hester Mulso, M^rs Chapone. See note on Hester Mulso. Chapter II, n. 25.

Hannah More (1745–1833). Her first work, *Percy*, a tragedy, was performed in London in 1777. This was followed by *Poems* and *Sacred Dramas* (1785); *Thoughts on the importance of the Manners of the Great* (1788); *Village Politics* (1792); *Strictures on Female Education* (1799); *Coelebs* (1809); and various tracts, pamphlets, and poems that appeared at intervals up to the end of her life.

Mary Granville (M^rs Pendarves, M^rs Delany) (1700–1788). She married Swift's friend, Patrick Delany, Dean of Down, for her second husband in 1743. Her *Autobiography* was begun in the form of Letters to the Duchess of Portland in 1740. Her *Essay on Propriety* was written in 1778. Her *Flora* was made between the years 1772 and 1785.

garded as authoritative nowadays. Even in her own day it won only guarded praise from Shakespearian critics: Johnson spoke of it with contempt and Maurice Morgann's comment, though more polite, is still ironical. But with a large public in England and in France it had a reception that was flattering enough, and its author's reputation as a Shakespearian scholar was established. She was the great Mrs Montagu to the end of her days. The fact that she added to this reputation an enormous income from her husband's coal mines enabled her to keep up her character of "female wit" in the grand style. Fanny Burney gives us a picture of her as she was in 1778—already a woman in middle life with a "sensible and penetrating countenance, and the air and manner of a woman accustomed to being distinguished and of great parts," and she adds, rather wickedly, "Dr Johnson who agrees in this, told us that a Mrs Harvey, of his acquaintance, says, she can remember Mrs Montagu *trying* for this same air and manner."[5] We see her again in the diarist's pages graciously offering her patronage to the young author of *Evelina*, as from superior heights. "If Miss Burney does write a play, I beg I may know of it; or if she thinks proper, see it; and all my influence is at her service,"[6] and Fanny Burney, though she never really liked Mrs Montagu, could not help being flattered by her interest. Another young writer who was glad to accept her patronage was Hannah More—and it is she who describes for us the magnificence of the Adam house in Portman Square where the Queen of the Blues entertained the Queen of England and six princesses to breakfast. Here Hannah More herself sat down to dinner with Miss Carter, Dr Johnson, and Sir Joshua and went home to write with the warmest enthusiasm of her hostess. "Mrs Montagu . . . . is not only the finest genius but the finest lady I ever saw."[7] Here too, in 1791, there assembled seven hundred people, Horace Walpole among them, to see the magnificent feather hangings it had taken her so long to procure.[8] All accounts unite to give us one impression of her: a stately lady commanding respect rather than love, but most certainly commanding respect. Dr Johnson respected her, though he did quarrel with her for her partisanship of Lord Lyttle-

[5] Madame d'Arblay, *Diary*. I, p. 70.

[6] *Ibid.*, I, 76.

[7] Hannah More, *Memoirs*. 1837. (ed. William Roberts.) Vol. I, p. 53.

[8] Horace Walpole, *Letters*. (ed. Paget Toynbee.) XV, p. 1.

ton. M^rs Delany respected her though she did laugh at her "room of Cupidons"[9] and at the parade and ostentation of her large assemblies. Even M^rs Thrale, a woman temperamentally opposed to her, was forced to do justice to her qualities of mind. "M^rs Montagu was brilliant in diamonds, solid in judgment, critical in talk," she writes on one occasion[10] after being in company with her, summing up for us in a line the woman of fashion and woman of learning. We may not read M^rs Montagu nowadays, but we read of her in the pages of others. There we can realize still the force of her personality and know why her friendship meant so much to the young aspirant to literary fame.

A woman of a very different type was Elizabeth Carter, the friend and companion of M^rs Montagu for many years. Miss Carter was not a woman of wealth like M^rs Montagu. Even if she had been, she would not have had the same ambition to play the hostess and fine lady. She attended M^rs Montagu in England and journeyed abroad with her to the various spas in quest of health; but one cannot imagine that she entered as readily into the splendid entertainments of Hill Street and Portman Square. Miss Carter was much nearer to the type that we should today call "bluestocking" than any of the rest of the original *Bas Bleus*. She was a woman whose devotion to learning made her indifferent to the things that usually occupy the feminine mind. She did not care for dress—several times in her letters she alludes laughingly to her own out-of-fashion-ness: she had likewise no desire to change her single state. "Marriage," she writes, "is a very right scheme for everybody but myself."[11] Books and her friends made Miss Carter's world. She lived a dedicated life—rising early, taking regular exercise (she was one of the few eighteenth-century women who could walk), living by preference in retirement in the country, and reading insatiably. In the letters which she exchanged with Catherine Talbot up to the latter's death in 1769, we have preserved for us a record of what these ladies read. Catherine Talbot keeps her friend up to date in the after-supper readings which were a daily institution in Bishop Secker's house, and Miss Carter in her turn gives a faithful account of the latest books that have come her way. The reading lists of both ladies might put the professed

[9] For this incident see Madame d'Arblay, *Diary*. I, pp. 548–9.

[10] Madame d'Arblay, *Diary*. I, p. 325.

[11] Elizabeth Carter, *Letters to M^rs Montagu*. London, 1817. II, p. 281.

student to shame; but Miss Carter is sometimes too learned even for her correspondent. Homer, Cicero, Montaigne, Ariosto, Cervantes—these are only a few of the names gathered at random from Miss Carter's earlier letters. She was always fitting herself for fresh excursions into the field of knowledge. In the course of her life she attained to the mastery of Greek and Latin, of French, German, Italian, Spanish, and Portuguese, and even knew something of Hebrew and Arabic. When she met M[rs] Montagu in 1758, she was already known as the translator of Epictetus, as the author of poems and of other translations and as an occasional contributor to the *Rambler*. Perhaps it was this fame which first attracted M[rs] Montagu, with her infallible instinct for "lions," but there is no doubt that afterwards she came to value Miss Carter's friendship for its own sake. It is one of the attractive things about Miss Carter that she was beloved as well as admired. She has none of the bloodlessness often associated with the woman scholar, and if we find her occasionally overpious, as M[rs] Montagu did at times, and if we feel that her intellectual judgment was warped by moral prejudice, we have to remember that there she is at one with her age. There is no undercurrent of dislike or disapproval in what her contemporaries have to say about Elizabeth Carter. Fanny Burney, meeting her at Bath in 1780, records what seems to have been the general impression in her diary. "Really a noble looking woman," she writes.[12] "I never saw age so graceful in the female sex yet; her whole face seems to beam with goodness, piety and philanthropy." Without having an income of £7000 a year or a house in Portman Square, Miss Carter was as well respected by her age as M[rs] Montagu. As Hannah More said of her in her poem called "The Bas Bleu,"[13]

> Carter taught the female train
> The deeply wise are never vain.

The mention of Hannah More's poem leads us back to the original Bluestocking to whom the lines are dedicated, M[rs] Vesey. In the *Advertisement*, which precedes the poem, the author explains what was the nature of the Bluestocking gatherings as she knew them: "They were composed of persons in general distinguished for their rank, talents or respectable character, who met frequently

[12] Madame d'Arblay, *Diary*. I, p. 269.

[13] Hannah More, *Works*. New York. 1837. I, p. 15.

at M^rs^ Vesey's and at a few other houses, for the sole purpose of conversation and were different in no respect from other parties but that the company did not play at cards."[14] She goes on to add that in this company "learning was as little disfigured by pedantry, good taste as little tinctured by affectation . . . . as has perhaps been known in any society." The term "bluestocking" has changed in meaning since that time and often connotes the very things which Hannah More denies to M^rs^ Vesey's assemblies. We are apt to forget, too, that the original Bluestockings were men as well as women—Horace Walpole, Lord Lyttleton, and Lord Bath are some of the names which Miss More celebrates. M^rs^ Vesey herself was certainly as little as possible of the bluestocking in the modern sense of the word. She did not dabble in literature nor do we hear anything of unusual learning or powers of scholarship in her. Her great talent seems to have been the social art—the art of bringing the right people together. Fanny Burney, who was evidently a little disappointed in her, notes her skill in this particular: "She is an exceeding well-bred woman and of agreeable manners," she writes,[15] "but all her name in the world, must, I think, have been acquired by her dexterity and skill in selecting parties, and by her address in rendering them easy with one another —an art, however, that seems to imply no mean understanding." When, indeed, we consider the people whom M^rs^ Vesey did select and render easy with one another, we must agree with the statement that she had no mean understanding. She had mind enough, at least, to make M^rs^ Montagu and Miss Carter her friends. They pet her and call her "dear Sylph"; they talk to her as to a little child; but they are unquestionably fond of her. We are made to feel her charm through the affection of others for her; she is a "sweet," "engaging," unpractical being, who flits restlessly through the assemblies and conversation, her fancy flying off already to plan her next party, while the present one is successfully in progress. M^rs^ Vesey was no Greek scholar or Shakespearian critic, but she must have the credit for achieving a great revolution in the world of drawing-room society—for it was she who first broke up the circle and instituted the group as the unit of conversation.

> Small was the art which would ensure
> The circle's boasted quadrature!

[14] *Ibid.*, p. 14.

[15] Madame d'Arblay, *Diary.* I, p. 166.

> See Vesey's plastic genius make
> A circle every figure take;[16]

so wrote Hannah More, who considered the innovation, as most people would, a blessing. Dr Johnson preferred his circle still, and, if there were always a Johnson to preside, we might even now be willing to follow the old method. As it is, we owe a vote of thanks to Mrs Vesey for being the first to introduce a convenient and comfortable arrangement.

It would take too long to make a sketch of all the great women of the period. Some like Mrs Vesey owe their fame to their social gifts and to their amiable personalities. Such was Mrs Ord, whose assemblies rivalled Mrs Vesey's; such, indeed, was Mrs Thrale. Some, like Mrs Cholmondeley and Mrs Walsingham, won, by their conversation, the name of "wit." Some, without this brilliance, enjoyed high reputations on their fine-ladyhood alone: such were Mrs Crewe and "highbred elegant Boscowen." There were poets among them like Fanny Greville, author of the "Ode to Indifference"; and playwrights, like Mrs Cowley who wrote the "Belle's Stratagem." Nor was literature the only art they followed, for we must not forget Mrs Sheridan, the "nightingale of Bath," nor Mrs Garrick, the lovely "Violetta," who was one of Fanny Burney's earliest heroines. In the little poem called *Advice to the Herald*,[17] which appeared in the *Morning Herald* for March 12, 1782, in which the names of "such as shine their sex's glory" are preserved for us, there are two which deserve special notice.

One of these is Mrs Chapone, whose *Letters on the Improvement of the Mind* was a book which many mothers of the age placed in the hands of their daughters.

> Or mark, well pleased, Chapone's instructive page
> Intent to raise the morals of the age,[18]

writes Hannah More, and there is no doubt that the age thought highly of her. Good sense is the quality with which her own contemporaries always credit her; good sense is what strikes us today when we read her *Letters*. She is not brilliant, she is not even very interesting, but she is intelligent and well informed; she is the sort of woman who would be an addition to any society but never the leader of it. For us her main interest lies in her association, first

[16] Hannah More, *Works*. I, p. 16.

[17] Quoted in Madame d'Arblay, *Diary*. I, p. 423. n.

[18] Hannah More, *Works*. I, p. 33.

with Richardson and later with the men and women of Johnson's circle. She is noteworthy as a good type of sensible educated woman, and a type that became increasingly common as the eighteenth century progressed. The second of these and the greater is Hannah More, whom it would be unpardonable to dismiss in a few lines, were it not for the fact that her greatest activity as a social worker and writer came later than the period under discussion. Hannah More was a younger woman than the original Bluestockings—twenty-five years younger than Miss Carter. Her "Bas Bleu" really celebrated a passing age and her attitude to the "old wits" is one of veneration. One cannot regard her as on terms of equality with the ladies to whose assemblies she was admitted. In the days when she flattered Dr Johnson and attended Mrs Montagu's salons, Hannah More was only feeling for her true vocation. The "pathetic pen" which the author of "*Advice to the Herald*" celebrates was not the pen that made the Bishop of London write to her in later days, "No age ever owed more to a female pen than yours."[19]

It is not unfitting to approach these eighteenth century women from the angle of the youthful author of *Evelina* and see who were the ones who counted most with her. Mrs Thrale, perhaps, was the one for whom she had most affection; and with her she was on terms of greater intimacy than with any of the others. Mrs Montagu, as we have seen, she valued for her influence and Miss Carter's acquaintance, too, she considered as an honour. But what she herself seems to regard as her greatest triumph was her introduction to Mrs Delany—the wonderful old lady who had been the friend of Swift, knew Richardson and Johnson and outlived them all. "Delany too is ours," writes Hannah More, in *Sensibility*, after enumerating the acknowledged female wits of the time—Mrs Montagu, Miss Carter, and Mrs Chapone—but it is not with these that Mrs Delany must be classed. She was the friend of all of them, it is true—she was even intimate enough with Mrs Montagu, in her youth, to have the privilege of calling that stately lady "Fidget"—but it is not as a "wit," not as a scholar, not as a Bluestocking that we remember her. She wrote an *Autobiography*, but she was too well-bred to write a good one; she wrote an *Essay on Propriety*, but this, while it fits in perfectly with her character, would not have been enough in itself to give her fame. Nor is it

[19] Hannah More, *Memoirs*. II, p. 52.

alone on her fine handwork—the needlework and shellwork and the unique *Flora*, that is preserved in the British Museum, that her reputation is founded. It is rather on herself—the sum total of the effect of her personality on all who come in contact with her. If she had not left us a line of her own writing, she would survive in the opinions of others. Fanny Burney, to whom she was something like a saint, speaks of her always with peculiar tenderness. "Benevolence, softness, piety and gentleness are all resident in her face," she writes on meeting her for the first time.[20] Hannah More celebrates her in verse that is commonplace enough, but that still shows a certain justness in the choice of epithets.

> Delany, too, is ours, serenely bright,
> Wisdom's strong ray and virtue's milder light,
> And she who blest the friend and grac'd the page
> Of poignant Swift, still gilds our social days.
> Long, long protract thy light, O star benign,
> Whose setting beams with milder lustre shine.[21]

Most of all she lives in Burke's famous saying that "M^rs^ Delany was the highest bred woman in the world and the woman of fashion of all ages." But besides the opinions of others we have her own *Letters* to make us acquainted with her. Here is none of the conscious brilliance of M^rs^ Montagu, none of the bookishness of Miss Carter. M^rs^ Delany was widely read, but she was not a "learned lady": she had humour, but she was not a "wit." In passing to her letters from those of the Bluestockings we enter a new atmosphere, one of greater ease and familiarity. Where Miss Carter spent her time inveighing against Voltaire's heretical opinions, or comparing the English and French philosophies, M^rs^ Delany writes delightfully of the Duchess of Queensberry's new gown or her own "new pussy." Even the pheasant she had for dinner or the roast onion she ate for supper are not too low and trivial to be subjects for her correspondence. It is people who count with her rather than books—and the dispositions and manners of people rather than their minds. It is characteristic of her that she preferred the "informing elegant" conversation of Queen Charlotte to M^rs^ Montagu's best sallies. She was herself above all things a "person," to be ranked with those whom Charles Lamb distinguished by the name. She was a person, moreover, to whom

[20] Madame d'Arblay, *Diary*. I, p. 515.
[21] Hannah More, *Works*. I, p. 33.

the greatest men in the land deferred and for whom the king himself placed her chair. And personality such as she possessed is a rarer thing than a talent for writing. The position of the Bluestockings is less secure, for all their printed pages, than that of the "highest bred woman in the world."

Enough has been said to show that Fanny Burney made her entrance into a different world from that of Sarah Fielding. It was a world by no means unfavourable to the woman writer. At its head was Johnson, who, remembering the time "when a woman who could spell a common letter was regarded as all accomplished,"[22] looked with great satisfaction on the progress made by women in literature and in learning. Johnson still maintained that man's was the superior mind. "It is plain, Madam," he said to M^rs^ Knowles,[23] "one or other must have the superiority. As Shakespeare says 'If two men ride a horse, one must ride behind' "; and there was no question in his mind that it was woman who must ride behind. But he was nevertheless feminist enough to disconcert Boswell by his "advanced" views. It is Boswell who rounds off the debate with M^rs^ Knowles, "that in another world the sexes will be equal." "That is being too ambitious, Madam," replies Boswell. "*We* might as well desire to be equal with the angels." That is a remark which Johnson would never have made. Education was still not a common enough advantage, nor writing a common enough pursuit among women for either to be taken for granted by the world. There is a little conscious superiority on the part of the Bluestockings and a little hostility on the part of those outside the circle, which show they were not regarded as a natural product of the times. Learning was still looked upon as somewhat unfeminine. M^rs^ Chapone in her *Letters* advises the young lady for whom she is writing, against the classical languages because they are likely to breed "pedantry and presumption in a woman" and make her the cause of "envy in the one sex and jealousy in the other."[24] Fanny Burney, too, is rather hurt at being accused of a knowledge of Latin. "I wonder, my dear Susy, what next will be said of me," is her comment to her sister on the occasion.[25]

[22] Madame d'Arblay, *Diary*. I, p. 160.

[23] Boswell, *Life of Johnson*. III, p. 326.

[24] M^rs^ Chapone, *Letters on the Improvement of the Mind*. Boston, (No date—ed. William Green.) II, p. 193.

[25] Madame d'Arblay, *Diary*. I, p. 133.

As regards authorship, M^rs^ Montagu herself shows us that she had her doubts about the propriety of publication. In a letter to her father-in-law, written in 1769, the year of her *Essay on Shakespeare*, she says: "When I was young, I should not like to have been classed among authors, but at my age, it is less unbecoming. If an old woman does not bewitch her neighbour's cows, nor make any girl in the parish spit crooked pins, the world has no reason to take offence at her amusing herself with reading books or even writing them."[26] "Amusing herself" is still the woman's only justification for writing and literature still the affair of the amateur. But in the age of Johnson, nevertheless, the woman author had many opportunities, which, in some ways, she has never had again, in the conversation and society of a number of unusually brilliant and gifted men and women.

## 2. Frances Burney, Madame d'Arblay, 1752–1840

Those who see in the progress of women's education the sole cause of their advance in literature must be content to lay aside their theories in the case of Fanny Burney. She had no regular education. While her brothers went at the usual age to a Public School and her elder and younger sisters were "finished" at Madame St. Mart's establishment in Paris, Fanny was left to pick up knowledge as best she could in the house and garden at Lynn Regis, where the first eight years of her life were passed, and later in her father's library in London. She was naturally slow to learn. She was eight years old before she knew her letters and ten before she learned to write. But before she could write, she had composed plays and speeches, and, before she had begun in earnest to read, she had embarked on her career as a writer of stories. Here is early evidence of the nature of her gifts—a power of observation and of remembering and recording impressions that did not depend on book learning. The education which Miss Burney afterwards gave herself, in her wide, uncritical reading, acted rather as a ballast than as a formative influence. It was not books that made her, but contact with people.

For contact with people—people of all ranks and types—she could not have been more happily situated. She possessed a father who was not only an eminent musician but one of the most beloved

[26] M^rs^. Montagu, Unpublished letter quoted by R. Huchon in *M^rs^ Montagu and her Friends*. p. 148.

of men. D^r^ Johnson's opinion of Charles Burney is well known: "I love Burney," he said. "My heart goes out to meet him . . . . D^r^ Burney is a man for all the world to love." Whether for love of D^r^ Burney or love of music, all the world seemed to gravitate to the Burney's London home. There was no lack of distinguished company in the not very fashionable neighbourhoods where Fanny Burney grew up—Poland Street, first, in the tall old house, next the wig-maker's, where she wrote and burned her earliest novels; then Queen Square in Alderman Barber's house, where at some time M^rs^ Manley must have lived with her benefactor; lastly St. Martin's Street, in the house that had belonged to Sir Isaac Newton. In Poland Street, Fulke Greville, the man of fashion who had chosen D^r^ Burney as companion in his youth, came often to sup and sometimes brought his wife, the beautiful Fanny Greville who was Fanny Burney's godmother. In Queen Square, on one "most heavenly evening," Fanny Burney heard Sacchini play on the harpsichord his own compositions, heard Celestin play his violin, and Millico, "the divine Millico," sing airs from Italian opera. In St. Martin's Street the great Agujari came to tea and sang again and again, before her informal audience. It was here, too, that M^r^ Garrick, a frequent visitor, gave "imitations" to amuse the young Burneys in their father's study. It was a brilliant company, indeed, that Fanny Burney kept in her youth—Russian princes, French Ambassadors, Danish Barons were no extraordinary events in St. Martin's Street—but, as she wrote to Susan in 1777, "Nobody suspects the brilliancy of the company I occasionally keep."[27] This was after she had created a society of her own in *Evelina*.

Fanny Burney may have been slow to learn in some ways, but she shows herself precocious enough in her interest in the romance of real life. As we have seen, she began to write at an early age—a habit which distressed her stepmother and brought about the conflagration in which these early masterpieces, the *History of Caroline Evelyn* among them, perished. After that, for several years, all her powers of composition were concentrated on her *Journals* and *Letters*. The psychological value of these will be discussed in another place, and all we need say about them at present is that they formed a practice ground for the young author between the period of the bonfire in Poland Street and the time

[27] Frances Burney, *Early Diary*. 1907. (ed. Annie Raine Ellis.) II, p. 150.

when the composition of *Evelina* was begun in secret. In 1778, when Miss Burney was twenty-six, *Evelina* was ready for publication. The intense secrecy which was preserved over the publication of this novel, the persistent manner in which Fanny guarded her anonymity, her halting confession to her father, before she carried her manuscript to the publisher, of what she was about to commit—all these things indicate that Fanny Burney was by no means anxious to be known to the world as a novelist. But we can make too much of this, in regarding as a sign of the times what was largely due to personal diffidence. Fanny Burney was known to be unusually bashful and retiring. Afterwards, when her reputation was established, and there was no doubt as to the reception which would be accorded to the author of *Evelina,* she was still distressed at being singled out in public. She did not wish to be conspicuous in any way or in any company, and it is conceivable that a woman of her age, today, might go through the same sensations over the publication of a first novel. The fact that she published at all without need, that she took her manuscript to Lowndes when Dodsley refused it, that her father received her confession only with good-natured amusement, are indications that the position of women novelists was no longer one to be ashamed of. Indeed, the atmosphere of excitement into which the whole family was thrown tends to show that they were, rather, proud of the woman novelist in their midst. After the reviews were out and judgment passed on it, there is no doubt as to their pride.

It is not too much to say that *Evelina* is the first book with which the woman novelist came into her own. The respectability of her calling had been established thirty years before, when gentlewomen of the type of Sarah Fielding and Charlotte Lennox began to write. These ladies had their followers in the Burneys' own circle. Frances Sheridan, mother of Richard Brinsley Sheridan, wrote novels if undistinguished ones; and Frances Brooke, wife of the Rev. John Brooke and a friend of Johnson's, was called by the *Gentleman's Magazine* "so distinguished a novelist that whatever she writes will be read with avidity."[28] These two at least must have

[28] Frances Moore, Mrs Brooke (1724–1789) was the author of several plays and novels, editor of a weekly paper, the *Old Maid,* which began in 1755, and joint manager of the King's Theatre in the Haymarket, after 1781, in association with Mrs Yates, the actress. Her best known novels are *Lady Julia Mandeville* (1763); *Emily Montagu* (1769); *The Excursion* (1777). It is the last named which is reviewed in the *Gentleman's Magazine* for 1777. (p. 387.)

been well known to Fanny Burney. But while the woman novelist was tolerated and taken for granted by this time, she has no positive position till after *Evelina.* It is easy to see why. It was not that Fanny Burney by any personal dignity or rank conferred an honour on her calling; it was chiefly that *Evelina* happened to be a good deal better novel than any written by a woman before it. It was so much better that Mr Brimley Johnson, in his work on *Women Novelists,* sweeps away all that went before it, and calls Miss Burney the first woman novelist. *Evelina* was fortunate, too, in the time of its appearance. Sarah Fielding and Charlotte Lennox had Richardson, Fielding, Smollett, and Sterne to contend with, as Jane Austen afterwards had Scott for a rival. Even a decade before *Evelina* might have had attention distracted from it by the *Sentimental Journey* or the *Vicar of Wakefield,* but, as it happened, it was the book not only of the year but of ten years. *Humphrey Clinker,* seven years before, had marked the passing of the four great novelists of the century, and they had left no worthy successors. All these circumstances united to put Miss Burney in a unique position. Add to the fact that she had written a good novel, at a time when good novels were scarce, the fact that she was a woman and young and Dr Burney's daughter into the bargain, and one sees why she came in for more than her share of praise. Jane Austen was less favoured in the reception given to her better novels—for she wrote in an age of good novels, nor did she move in a circle "where everybody's somebody."

The first volume of the *Diary of Madame d'Arblay* is a record of the young author's triumphal progress. It is like another novel of which Fanny Burney herself is the heroine. We begin with its effect on her own family. Susan, of course, who was early in the secret, admired it immensely and only wished the rumour were true which credited her with a hand in it. It is Susan who breaks the news to her sister that Dr Burney is reading *Evelina* and liking it "vastly"; and that he is reading it aloud, moreover, to some ladies of his acquaintance who are in raptures over it. Later when Dr Burney has finished the book, he gives it as his opinion that it is the best novel he ever read except Fielding's. Praise such as this from her father was enough to satisfy Fanny Burney, but it was only the beginning of her success. From her own family circle we pass next to the reading of *Evelina* at Chesington—the home of Mr Crisp, her second "daddy," and witness the poor author's sufferings when she has to listen to speculations on the possible authorship of her own book. "'Tis the sweetest book," says one,[29] "don't you think so, Miss Burney?" and "A'n't you sorry this sweet book is done?" asks another. She is happy that her book was always a "sweet book" to the readers and that she never had to listen to adverse criticism of the unknown author. There is no doubt, either, that she got a good deal of amusement out of this innocent mystification to make up for the embarrassment she suffered in hearing herself discussed.

"Take care of your head," said Dr Burney to his daughter when he wrote to tell her how vastly delighted Mrs Thrale and Dr Johnson were with *Evelina*. When we go on to read of compliments that showered upon Miss Burney once her identity was known, we do not wonder that her father found the injunction necessary. She was "almost craz'd" when she heard of Dr Johnson's approbation, but in the years she lived with Mrs Thrale at Streetham she had to get used to hearing her praises sung by Johnson and many another. It is remarkable, indeed, that she kept her head so well, for everyone she met seemed in league to turn it for her. To be told that Burke had sat up all night to finish her book and that Sir Joshua was "mad about it"[30] and would give fifty pounds to know the author was enough to spoil a young author at the outset, and Fanny Burney felt the danger of being spoilt. When Dr Johnson said in her presence, "I admire her for her observation, for her good sense, for her humour, for her discernment, for her manner of expressing them and for all her writing talents,"[31] it is no wonder that she sighed with "mixed gratitude for the present and apprehension for the future." To have Murphy and Sheridan begging her to write a comedy and offering to take up anything she wrote unseen, to listen to Mrs Cholmondeley's boisterous compliments and Dr Warton's more delicate praise, in a single evening—all this was a preparation for the life she lived in the years after the publication of *Evelina*, when she was Mrs Thrale's companion. It is the same tale wherever she goes—Tunbridge, Brighthelmstone, or Bath. Great wits extend their patronage to her, and lesser wits sue for her patronage. No book by a woman

[29] For this incident see Madame d'Arblay, *Diary*, I, pp. 12–13, and *Letters from Susan to Frances Burney* in *Early Diary*. II.

[30] *Diary*. I, p. 64.

[31] *Ibid.*, p. 69.

ever, like *Pamela*, set the church bells ringing, but *Evelina* came nearer to it than any.

Fanny Burney's fame in her own day was increased by *Cecilia* in 1782, and the compliments begin afresh from her old admirers. There were few worlds left for her to conquer, but it was pleasant nevertheless to hear that Queen Charlotte admired the book, that M^rs^ Delany was reading it, and that the Duchess of Portland, who could not read *Clarissa*, had read *Cecilia* through three times. It was after *Cecilia* that "little Burney's quick discerning" was celebrated in the *Advice to the Herald*, already referred to. "Do you know they have put me again into the newspapers," she writes to Susan,[32] "in a copy of verses made upon literary ladies—where are introduced M^rs^ Carter, Chapone, Cowley, Hannah More, M^rs^ Greville, M^rs^ Boscowen, M^rs^ Thrale, M^rs^ Crewe, Sophy Streatfield and M^rs^ Montagu? In such honourable company, to repine at being placed, would, perhaps be impertinent, so I take it quietly enough; but I would to Heaven I could keep clear of the whole." Her wish was soon to be gratified, for her fame as a literary lady was almost over. In 1784 the death of D^r^ Johnson and the marriage of M^rs^ Thrale with Piozzi broke up the circle at Streatham. The end of the first volume of the *Diary* is the end of the brilliant period of Fanny Burney's life. In the next year began the long exile at Court, where the genteel commonplaces of Queen Charlotte's conversation, the chat of the equerries, and the silence of M^rs^ Schwellenberg were all her substitute for the wit and good sense of the men and women she had met in Johnson's society. After M^rs^ Delany's death in 1788, the tedium of her existence as Maid of Honour must have been insupportable. When she emerged from her seven years of court life, the scene was changed. The old wits were passing, many of them already dead. Her marriage with General d'Arblay begins a new phase in her life and *Camilla* in 1793 was written more out of need than out of any ambition to continue, as Madame d'Arblay, the literary reputation of Miss Burney. Once the d'Arblays were established in "Camilla Cottage" with their garden and a new circle of acquaintances, Fanny Burney the novelist was dead. Her last attempt at fiction, *The Wanderer*, in 1814, was a failure, and the only literary work which Madame d'Arblay undertook for the rest of her life was the editing of her father's *Memoirs* and the compiling of her own. The end

[32] *Ibid*, p. 422.

of Fanny Burney's life is a disappointment after its brilliant start. How much the deadening life at Court is to blame for the change, and how much it was due to a natural exhaustion of the original spring of genius that made *Evelina* is a matter for psychologists to decide. One can make out a case for her happy marriage with d'Arblay as the cause—for it is a fact worth noting that the successful woman writer, as a rule, is either a spinster or a widow. Mrs Behn, Mrs Manley, and Mrs Haywood were widows who never achieved a settled domestic calm, Pènelope Aubin wrote after hèr widowhood and Charlotte Lennox wrote chiefly before her marriage and after the death of her husband. Sarah Fielding and Jane Barker were unmarried women—the latter, at least, an unwilling spinster whose past unhappy love affair was the making of her books. Of the women of Johnson's circle Miss Carter and Miss More were never married, Mrs Montagu's marriage was one of convenience, and Mrs Chapone's married life lasted only ten months. Whether there is any truth in the theory or not, it is undoubtedly true that the interest in Fanny Burney is almost over when she becomes Madame d'Arblay. She lived on to become an Early Victorian, but the important period in her life and in the history of the woman novelist is the period from *Evelina* to *Çecilia*.

## 3. New Tendencies in the Novel

Fanny Burney's career shows the woman novelist at last in an assured position, achieved by a happy combination of natural gifts and favouring circumstances. Had Miss Burney been a provincial miss, her triumph would have been less glorious; had *Evelina* been an inferior novel, it would never have passed the critics. As it was, Miss Burney put beyond a doubt the propriety of her calling. In Richardson's day the "lady novelist" still had doubts as to the suitability of appearing in print: Richardson himself, while lamenting the loss of possible masterpieces, held back from the world by female nicety, could not blame the authors for their scruples. "Till this world is mended," he writes,[33] "a lady perhaps may be justified in fearing lest she should be looked upon (as Harriet says) 'like an owl among birds' . . . . I think the present more liberal education of our girls may probably pave the way for their emancipation hereafter: but in the meantime I acknowledge, I cannot from my heart blame those who are afraid

[33] Richardson, *Correspondence.* III, p. 89.

of being made the jest of fools for performances above their comprehension." Sarah Fielding had felt the need of apology and Lady Wortley Montagu is heartily sorry that her kinswoman should be driven by necessity to write novels for a living. The patronage of men of letters and of Johnson in particular had done much to raise the literary reputation of women like Charlotte Lennox, but it did not confer social prestige. Johnson's friendship meant a good deal, but it was no passport to the fashionable part of society, for his acquaintance embraced all ranks from George III down to Bet Flint. But Fanny Burney had the freedom of both communities—the world of letters and of fashion. Once she had been well received, no lady of high society was afraid to acknowledge her own manuscripts. Elegant amateurs like Lady Hawke, author of the *Mausoleum of Julia*[34] came forward to claim Miss Burney as a sister authoress. The *Mausoleum of Julia*, alas, is lost to us, all but the one "sweet part" which the author is persuaded to repeat aloud by her sister, Lady Sele and Say, (though we have her word for it that "it's all just like that part"); but the scene remains, one of the most inimitable in Madame d'Arblay's *Diary*, to show us that the support of a new type of person is enlisted on behalf of the woman writer. Lady Sele and Say, as described by Fanny Burney, is an incredibly stupid woman, but she belonged to a class of society whose patronage had more weight than it deserved. When she exclaims in admiration, "I can't think how you can write these sweet novels," Fanny Burney might laugh at her in private, but she would have admitted that her position was more comfortable than that of her predecessors, for whom High Society had nothing but contempt.

Fanny Burney made it clear to the critics, also, that a woman was capable of writing a work of genius. *Evelina* may owe a good deal to the novels that went before it, but it is not an imitative work. It is sprung from those earlier works that were burned in the yard at Poland Street, and these were written before the author had read many novels of any kind. It is to the credit of the reviewers that they recognized her originality. She had written not only a good novel, but a novel different from anything that went before it. Henceforth it could be no surprise to find women striking out on lines of their own, and the opinion was no longer justifiable

[34] Madame d'Arblay, *Diary*. I, 411 etc.

that the woman author was only following, at a respectful distance, in the path of the men.

One thing that still remained for the woman author was to achieve independence by her work. No woman novelist hitherto had managed to live entirely on what she could get by her writing, though it was need that made women take to authorship as a career in the first place. Those who had been most successful from a pecuniary standpoint had relied on what they wrote for the stage, rather than upon what they wrote for the mere reader. Literature was still the affair of the amateur or of the Grub Street drudge though conditions were beginning to change towards the end of Johnson's career. Men, as well as women, had to wait before the spread of education created a wider circle of readers and a demand for books which realized itself in money. Hannah More, coming up from Bristol to London with the conventional tragedy in her pocket, shows a new spirit of independence in setting out to seek literary fame; but her fortune she did not have to seek. A woman who really made herself independent was Elizabeth Inchbald,[35] the author of *A Simple Story*, who ran away from her home in Norwich to become an actress in London, and led a life as adventurous as the heroine of any novel. But we cannot say that it was as a novelist alone that she achieved her independence—she was an actress and dramatist besides and probably found these more immediate appeals to the public more profitable than her *Simple Story* or *Nature and Art*. Charlotte Smith,[36] in the closing years of the century, by continual hard work and a prolific output of novels, poems, and translations managed to keep herself and her children and even help her shiftless husband out of what she made by her pen. All these facts are important as attempts on the part of women to become free. On the other hand, they show liter-

[35] Elizabeth Simpson, Mrs Inchbald (1753–1821) went to London in 1772 to become an actress and married Mr Inchbald soon afterwards. After his death in 1779, she wrote for the stage and her first play was acted in 1784. *A Simple Story* was published in 1790 and *Nature and Art* in 1796.

[36] Charlotte Turner, Mrs Smith (1749–1806) was married in 1765 to Benjamin Smith against her inclination. She and her husband were both imprisoned for debt in 1782 and it was after this that she began to write for a livelihood. In 1784 she published a book of poems, which was followed by her novels: *Emmeline* (1788), *Ethelinde* (1790), *Desmond* (1792), and the *Old Manor House* (1793). She wrote other novels, poems, and translations up to the time of her death, but these are her best-known works.

ary ability made subservient to the pressure of necessity. It is not until we come to George Eliot that we find a woman who consciously fitted herself for a literary career and lived by what she wrote, without sacrificing her best powers to the exigencies of the moment.

One woman, however, who might have made a fortune by her novels at the end of the eighteenth century was Ann Radcliffe. The quietness of M^rs^ Radcliffe's own life, in contrast with the scenes she writes of, has always impressed her critics and biographers. Ann Ward, born in London in 1764, entered after a calm, ordinary childhood and youth, upon a calm, ordinary married life by her marriage with William Radcliffe in 1787. She might have had opportunities of going into distinguished society, for at the house of her aunt she met several of the celebrities associated with Fanny Burney—M^rs^ Piozzi, M^rs^ Ord, and even M^rs^ Montagu herself. But she does not seem to have wished to cultivate their friendship and, later in life, when Miss Carter, who admired her writings, tried to make her acquaintance at Bath, she found M^rs^ Radcliffe obdurate in refusing to enter into company. Bred up in the tradition of female accomplishment, to the idea that "nothing lovelier can be found in woman than to study household good," Ann Radcliffe steadily declined to become a celebrity. At the height of her fame she ceased to publish altogether. Whether this was because she feared publicity or because, after her father's death in 1798, she was too much occupied in managing the estate in Leicestershire that came to her by his will, we have no means of finding out. All we know is that while she lived in Bath, in the centre of a society that would have lionized her, she carefully cut herself off from any such possibility.

M^rs^ Radcliffe began to write, in the first place, to beguile the long evenings, while her husband was absent in connection with his editorial work on the *British Chronicle.* Her first work, the *Castles of Athlin and Dunbayne*, published anonymously in 1789, passed without much comment from the critics or the public. The *Sicilian Romance*, in the next year, excited more curiosity. Miss Carter expresses her admiration for its elegance of language, exquisite painting of scenery, and originality of plot, in a letter to M^rs^ Montagu, from whom she is trying to find out the name of the author. It was, however, *The Romance of the Forest*, in 1791, which made M^rs^ Radcliffe famous, and her fame was increased by *Udol-*

*pho*, in 1794, and *The Italian*, in 1797. For the last two works her pecuniary reward was great. *Udolpho* brought her £500 and *The Italian* £800 from the booksellers—unprecedented prices for a woman's work in those days, and good prize-money even today. The sum paid for *The Italian* was greater than that which Millar paid for *Tom Jones* and, had Mrs Radcliffe cared to go on publishing, there is every chance that her next book would have equalled *Amelia's* record of £1000. But she did not choose. The poems of her latter years and the romance of *Gaston de Blondeville*, published in 1826, three years after her death, were never intended for the press. While her contemporary, Charlotte Smith, was trying all means to hit the public taste and make a living for her family, Mrs Radcliffe, who had the secret of pleasing her readers in her power, preferred to put an end to her literary career. There is no reason to think that her powers were exhausted or that the public was satiated with what she gave them. But at least she saved herself from the danger of an anticlimax.

It is not only for the large sums which her works brought her that we have to notice Mrs Radcliffe. She is notable as a woman who led the way for other novelists and in more than one direction. As Sir Walter Scott said of her in his *Lives of Eminent Novelists*: "She has taken the lead in a line of composition appealing to those powerful and general sources of interest, a latent sense of supernatural awe and curiosity concerning whatever is hidden and mysterious."[38] In this she was not entirely original. She took a hint from Walpole's *Castle of Otranto* and a hint from Clara Reeve's *Old English Baron*, which had been published in 1777. But, more than either of these, she has mastered the art of touching her readers' nerves. A book in which the appeal is to the nerves is surer of popularity than one which appeals either to heart or head. Its popularity may be brief, its charm may be gone after a single reading, but, for the moment, the appeal is certain. It is one which a wider circle of readers is capable of feeling and one which high and low in the intellectual scale find irresistible. Mrs Radcliffe was an early master of the ghost story. Though our taste today may have been spoiled for her mysteries by the more subtle ghosts of modern fiction, read in the right circumstances she can still raise a thrill in some readers and those who are too hardened for this, must, at least, see the fascination she had for her own age.

[37] Scott, *Lives of Eminent Novelists*. p. 578.

Horace Walpole must have the credit for the first mystery novel in the English language, but his management of the supernatural is far less effective than Mrs Radcliffe's. Clara Reeve,[38] in writing her *Old English Baron*, protested against the improbability of Walpole's story, and Scott, in his life of Clara Reeve, attacked her on this point. "If we are to try ghosts by the ordinary rules of humanity," he says,[39] "we bar them of their privileges entirely. For instance why admit the existence of an aerial phantom and deny it the terrible attribute of magnifying its stature? Why admit an enchanted helmet and not a gigantic one?" This is all perfectly logical, of course, but logic is out of place in the realm of the supernatural. Scott may have been able to take in just as much of illusion as he wanted, but the majority of readers would accept the aerial phantom, at its normal stature and refuse to believe in it when it magnified its size, would pass the helmet but stop at a gigantic one. There is a certain point at which human imagination stops short, even in a world admittedly unreal. We have no wish to try the poor ghost by the rules of ordinary life, but there are some things which we cannot "swallow." Most readers would support Clara Reeve against Scott in her objections to the extravagances of the *Castle of Otranto*. Clara Reeve's own tale of mystery, on the other hand, is hardly mysterious enough. Horace Walpole retorts to her criticism of his work by objecting to the mildness of hers. "It is so probable," he says,[40] "that any trial for murder at the Old Bailey would make a more interesting story," and one wonders, indeed, at the enthusiasm of Anna Seward, who professes to have read the *Old English Baron* repeatedly with "unsated pleasure."[41] Lord Lovel's ghost is the successor of those matter-of-fact mediaeval apparitions who walked the earth with a purpose and, when it was fulfilled, retired in peace to their graves. He is probable enough, but he does not chill the blood.

[38] Clara Reeve (1729–1807), daughter of a clergyman in Colchester, began her literary career with the *Phoenix* (1762), a translation of the Latin romance *Argenis*, and published in 1777 the *Old English Baron*, which was followed by other novels and semihistorical memoirs. Another ghost story, *Castle Connor* (1787), was lost in the post on its way to the publishers.

[39] *Ibid*., p, 547.

[40] Horace Walpole, *Letters*. (ed. Toynbee.) X, p. 217.

[41] *Gentleman's Magazine*. 1786. pp. 15–16. From a criticism of Clara Reeve's *Progress of Romance*.

One cannot imagine that either the *Castle of Otranto* or the *Old English Baron* kept even the readers of their own day from sleep, but one can see why M^rs^ Radcliffe sent girls like Catherine Morland to bed in a thrill of fear. She has the art of creating an atmosphere in which her readers are ready to expect anything. Where there is a lull in the hurried succession of events, there is always some hysterical servant to cry, "Hark, what is that?" and add the weight of her imaginary terrors to the graver fears we are already suffering for the heroine. When Henry Tilney exposes the artifices by which M^rs^ Radcliffe plays continually on her readers' nerves, it all seems ridiculous enough—the dilapidated castle, with its bloodstains and fluttering tapestries, its ancient domestics and secret passages; a place where the moon comes in through narrow casements, but never, it seems, the sun; where lamps expire always at the moment when there is most need of them; and where the poor heroine is invariably lodged in a different staircase from all the rest of the household. In all this we recognize the favorite stage effects of the melodrama and smile superior because we are no longer to be taken in by such tricks of the theatre. But to the eighteenth century they were not stock effects, but new and thrilling. It was not only girls like Catherine Morland who found *Udolpho* the "nicest book in the world": Joseph Warton, Headmaster of Winchester, sat up all night to read it, and Sheridan and Charles James Fox admired it. We have to admit, with Scott, that, in her own way, she was a master, and try to accept her mysteries in the spirit of an age which was not pampered with a new "thriller" in every week of the year.

As mysteries, M^rs^ Radcliffe's novels lose in the dénouement, when she begins to investigate the causes of the supernatural happenings and finds an explanation for events which we should have been perfectly willing to leave unexplained. Few readers will forgive her, in particular, for the heartless way in which she cheapens the secret of the veiled picture at the end of *Udolpho*. On the other hand, by postulating a reasonable explanation for the apparently inexplicable events of her narrative, she offers a new kind of pleasure to the reader. In an inconsequent story like the *Castle of Otranto*, no enjoyment can be derived from forming a personal theory as to how it will all end. All the pleasure is in surprise and not in expectation. In M^rs^ Radcliffe's novels, though it must be admitted that the far-fetched character of most of her explanations makes guesswork an unprofitable amusement, there is an opportunity for the alert reader to work out the solution of the mystery, along with the author. In this is the germ of the first detective stories. In *The Italian*,[41a] for instance, when Bianchi is discovered dead in her bed, her face overspread by a black tint—for this was none of your subtle poisons—the doctor, though he does not call the police, otherwise follows the correct procedure, by questioning the servants. "I wish to understand," he says to the maid, "what was the exact situation of this lady for some hours previous to her decease." So might Scotland Yard begin its investigations; nay, even Hercule Poirot or Philo Vance has to begin from some such preliminary. As for the scene in the vaults of the Holy Inquisition, melodramatic as it is and overfull of peripety and discovery, it is a prototype of all those scenes in coroners' courts and courts of law, which are the standby of the modern detective novelists. As one piece of evidence after another is brought forward, the reader finds himself compelled to form theories of his own to explain Schedoni, the hooded monk, and the strange connection between them. We must not make too much of this—Mrs Radcliffe's realm is the supernatural, and the presence of natural explanations is apt to spoil the unity of impression of the whole story— but a long line of popular fiction is descended from her early attempts, and, at least, she must have the credit for her originality.

In one other way Mrs Radcliffe comes forward as an innovator, and this is probably the most important of all her experiments—she was the first to introduce natural scenery, to any great extent, into the setting of her novels. The modification "to any great extent" is necessary because there had been hints in earlier novels of the appreciation of Nature. If we go as far back as *Oroonoko*, we find the scenes are enacted before a painted backcloth of vivid tropical landscape; but it is only in *Oroonoko* that Mrs Behn takes the trouble to describe her background. Perhaps she went into detail in this novel because the setting she described was new to her readers, and she liked to feel she was giving them information or to impress upon them more fully that she had been an eyewitness to these unusual happenings. Mrs Manley's descriptions of gardens and pleasure grounds are purely conventional. Her Nature is not Nature as she is, but the idealized Nature of Pastoral

[41a] Mrs Radcliffe, *The Italian*. p. 135.

romance—with its embroideries and enamellings, checkered shade, and undying flowers and a rain of blossoms perpetually falling like one of the "effects" of a ballet. Jane Barker, as we have seen, apologizes in her Preface for introducing the description of a garden into her *Entertaining Novels* but, as she justly adds, it will make no difference to the story if the reader prefers to leave it out; yet Jane Barker confesses elsewhere to a love of Nature which was a solace to her in the days of her unhappy love affair, and, had she cared to be a little more unconventional, she might have given us more of Nature in her novels than the geometrically laid out garden, which is merely idealized Ranelagh.

So far we do not find much evidence of natural description or appreciation of Nature in the eighteenth century novel. In *Felicia to Charlotte*, however, an epistolary novel published in 1744 by the little known Mary Mitchell Collyer,[42] we find enthusiastic descriptions of country landscape and of the joys of a rural life. The country of which Felicia writes to Charlotte is real country, though the author cannot rid herself entirely of the old phrases from pastoral poetry when she describes it. We recognize the English countryside with its violets and primroses and "rabbets scudding about." The editor assures us, moreover, that it is, indeed, drawn from life, in a footnote which he finds it necessary to append to the first letter in which natural scenery is described. "Lest this description should be thought romantic," it reads, "the editor thinks himself obliged to inform the public that this and the rest of the landscapes are actually situated near Nottingham." Evidently this was a new idea to the public, for whom landscapes situated near Nottingham had probably been thought too humble a subject by previous novelists. There is, however, no atmosphere about the scenic descriptions in Mrs Collyer's *Letters*. She writes as though she were giving directions to a landscape gardener, groves on the right, alleys on the left, vistas here, and arches there. She cannot put life into the scenes she describes, nor, though she loves Nature herself, convey her feelings to the reader.

[42] Mrs Mary Mitchell Collyer (1716–1762) translated Gesner's *Death of Abel* (1761) and Klopstock's *Messiah* (1762) besides writing the novel, *Felicia to Charlotte* 1744 and the *Christmas Box* 1749, a series of tales for children. Of her life we know practically nothing except that she was the wife of Joseph Collyer, a translator and printer. For the quotations from her novel I am indebted to an article by Helen Sard Hughes, *Journal of English and Germanic Philology*. XV, p. 645 etc.

The novels written by men during the same period are, on the whole, equally lacking in natural description. Richardson's scenes are laid, as a rule, indoors, and, when he does go out, he does not stop to notice the beauty of the park where Clarissa strolls, or the variety of the scenery through which Pamela makes her journey from Bedfordshire to Derbyshire. Fielding, while he can convey admirably the feeling of being out of doors, leaves us to imagine his background, for he does not paint it in. Perhaps it is, indeed, because he feels his readers would not appreciate it, rather than because he did not appreciate it himself, that he avoids description in his novels. Of the view which Tom Jones had, from the top of Mazard Hill at sunrise, he writes, "one of the most noble prospects in the world presented itself to their view and which we would likewise present to the reader, but for two reasons: first we despair of making those who have seen this prospect admire our description; secondly, we very much doubt whether those who have not seen it, would understand it."[43] We may accept these two reasons but might add to them a third—that Fielding's interest was in describing people and not scenery, and with his hero's fate yet undecided, he preferred to be carrying forward the action of the story. It is not until we come to Thomas Amory's *John Buncle*, 1766, that we find a novel which devotes much space to natural scenery. The part of the world which Amory chooses to describe is the English Lake country, through which John Buncle wanders in his search for one wife after another; and there is no doubt that the author had a real appreciation of the rugged beauty of the Cumberland landscape. But no north-countryman would recognize in Amory's fantastic canvases the scenes of his own home county. There is nothing specifically English in the wild country which he describes—indeed, the charming houses that sit perilously on the edge of frowning precipices might be called specifically un-English in their effect. But neither is John Buncle a specifically English character. For the "famous fine man formed in Nature's most eccentric hour" the author has had to find a famous, fine eccentric setting.

We cannot pretend, either, that the descriptions of natural scenery which occupy so much space in Mrs Radcliffe's novels are drawn from the actual landscapes. They took their colour

[43] Fielding, *Tom Jones.* (Everyman Edition.) I, p. 520.

from the extraordinary events for which they form a background. To heighten the feeling of mystery and romance, M[rs] Radcliffe deepens her lights and shadows, magnifies her heights and extends her distances. She did not know the country she was describing in *Udolpho*, the *Sicilian Romance*, or *The Italian*. As Miss Manwaring has pointed out, in her *Italian Landscape in England in the Eighteenth Century*, she was probably drawing a good deal from the landscape art of Salvator Rosa and Claude Lorrain. Many references to these artists show her familiar with their work, but, apart from that, there is a picturesque quality in her descriptions—I use the word literally—which suggests that she looked on Nature with the eye of the pictorial artist. Again and again we see her pictures through a frame—whether it be the narrow casement from which Emily looks out of the Castle of Udolpho, or an opening in the glade of the forest, through which Adeline sees a gentler landscape. It does not surprise us to know that M[rs] Radcliffe, like her heroines, had a very fair talent for drawing. She was also something of a poet. It is not the indifferent verse, scattered through her pages, that is a proof of this as much as the language of her prose descriptions and the feeling behind the whole. The poet in her made her idealize in her romances the scenes which she could describe faithfully, with her eye on the object, in her *Journals*. Her record of her tour through the South of England shows her a connoisseur in views no less than the descriptions of the grander scenery of the Apennines, but it shows also a truth to detail which is lacking in the novels. In a note on Rochester Castle, made in the September of 1797, we see the same taste which led her to draw her imaginary Castles, when she observes "its square ghastly walls and their hollow eyes, rising over a bank of the Medway, grey and massive and floorless." A jotting taken down in the following year, at Esher, suggests the less rugged scenes of the Gascon landscape round the home of the St. Auberts "Ascending to Esher by twilight, heard the bells sounding with most melancholy sweetness from the summit and strengthening as we approached: everything pensive and tranquil." No one can doubt, who reads the *Journals*, that the intensified landscapes of the novels are based on a genuine appreciation and knowledge of Nature. It is places and not people that M[rs] Radcliffe finds most worth while describing in her tours. She does not amuse herself, like Fanny Burney, with the eccentricities of the other visitors, nor does she record the domestic details of her accommodation, bills of fare, or conveniences of travel. Once, at Brighton, she stops to look at a cricket match on the sands, such as could never have taken place in Languedoc, but incidents like this are rare. Her enjoyment of Nature was one of the deepest things in her life, and she makes it an integral part of her novels. From the novels before her day one could eliminate the natural description, like Jane Barker's garden, and leave the books little the worse, but dislodge the Castle of Udolpho from its setting in the Apennines, remove the Abbey of St. Clare from Fontainville Forest and you have taken away half the novel. The reader may find the long descriptions wearisome, he may detect a lack of subtlety in the recurrence of certain rather grandiloquent words and phrases of which the writer is overfond—her favourite "eminences" and "edifices," the "horror" and "effulgence" without which no landscape is complete; but he cannot deny that in this branch of her art Mrs Radcliffe is immeasurably better than any of her predecessors in the English novel.

We must regard Mrs Radcliffe not only as a "best seller" of her own day but as a formative influence in the history of the novel. Once women have begun to lead the way, to strike out lines for themselves and point out new paths even to great men like Scott, there is no need for us to follow them any further. The woman novelist had ceased to be a phenomenon to excite surprise: the time when Mrs Radcliffe was writing there were many others in the field. Some of these we have already noticed. Clara Reeve in her *Old English Baron* made a contribution not only to the literature of the supernatural but to the historical romance of which the Waverley novels were the culmination. Charlotte Smith, in whose novels all the tendencies of the time appear but who is outstanding in no one thing, in *Desmond*, at least, makes the novel a means of airing her political views and was censured by Miss Carter for being "too favourable to democratic principles." The "novel with a purpose" was coming into being, and women were among the first to use it for the criticism of social, political, and religious institutions. Mary Wollstonecraft, whom one hardly thinks of as a novelist, wrote with deliberate purpose in *Mary. A Fiction* in 1788; and Mrs Inchbald, with a purpose of a different kind, in her *Simple Story* in 1791. All these women were trying experiments.

There are many other women novelists, who are only names to us. Mrs Brookes, for instance, was once part owner of the Opera House where her own plays were produced and a celebrated author to boot. She survives in the memoirs of the time as a woman of parts, though ill-favoured; but who now reads *Julia Mandeville* or *Emily Montagu*? Her contemporary, Frances Sheridan, has been kindlier treated by time, for she has only recently been resuscitated: first by an edition of her play *The Discovery* "mangled" by Mr Aldous Huxley for Sir Nigel Playfair and printed on Italian handmade paper, with a roseate cover; then again, by a similarly gorgeous limited edition of her little Arabian Nights story of *Nourjahad*. But not all the glory of Eastern illustrations and a stage *décor* in the manner of the "Lyric" Hammersmith can raise her from the dead. In the end she is only Sheridan's mother and the writer of an obscure comedy whose name appears in a list of Mr Huxley's works. Then there is Mrs Kier, author of the *History of Miss Greville*, which Miss Carter recommended to Mrs Montagu; or Mrs Griffiths, author of *Henry and Frances*, which Fanny Burney enjoyed in her youth. There are many who are not even names to most people. Who, for instance, has heard of the nine Miss Minifies?—a formidable literary family. Yet these ladies in their day were "reckoned ingenious"[44] and included in any list of "light summer reading." How many novels there were, which, like the *Mausoleum of Julia*, never saw the press at all, we can only guess at, but, from the works we have, and those whose names are recorded, we can see that the trade of novelist was no longer an uncommon one among women. It had come to be almost the first resort of the needy woman who fifty years before could hardly have lived by her pen and kept her character. After the turn of the century the output of novels by women is at least equal to that of the men, and if anything, it is the women who are more prolific. A publisher's announcement, picked out at random—it happens to be taken from the 1816 edition of Mrs Smith's *Emmeline*[45] in a list of eighteen novels has nine written by women as against five by men and four which are anonymous. In no other branch of literature do we find any record equal to this. It

[44] Elizabeth Carter, *Letters to Catherine Talbot*. 1809. III, p. 164 and note.

[45] Charlotte Smith, *Emmeline*. 1816. Fifth Edition. Volume II contains a list of New Publications for A. K. Newman & Co. at the Minerva Press, Leadenhall Street.

was the novel, before anything else, that brought the woman author before the public.

Between the years 1796 and 1799, Jane Austen was writing *Pride and Prejudice*, *Northanger Abbey*, and *Sense and Sensibility*. We cannot go into her career in detail for it was not until the second decade of the nineteenth century that her works appeared, and she is, besides, a subject for a thesis in herself. But she is the end to which we have been leading—the woman novelist who showed the heights which were capable of being reached by her sex, and for whom the earlier writers were unconsciously preparing the way. Jane Austen wrote, we are told, in the family sitting room and on scraps of paper. She wrote, like M^rs^ Behn, amid the conversation of others. But this does not mean that she adopted a casual attitude towards her art. In *Northanger Abbey*, she has her fling at the opinion which still persisted—and still, one might add, persists—that the novel is an inferior form of literature. " 'And what are you reading Miss?'—Oh! it is only a novel,' replies the young lady; while she lays down her book with affected indifference or momentary shame. 'It is only *Cecilia*, or *Camilla*, or *Belinda*'; or in short, only some work in which the greatest powers of the mind are displayed, in which the most thorough knowledge of human nature, the happiest delineation of its varieties, the liveliest effusions of wit and humour are conveyed to the world in the best-chosen language."[46] Here is praise, indeed, for the novelist and praise for Miss Burney and Miss Edgeworth in particular. Jane Austen was less kind to M^rs^ Radcliffe, but *Northanger Abbey* could not have been written without her, any more than the *Female Quixote* could have been written without the Scudérys. She is alive to the faults of her sister novelists, both of the school of "sensibility" and the school of "terror," but she was aware that women had made an important contribution to literature.

Jane Austen wrote with the idea of publication. She published, at first anonymously, but she does not seem to have suffered any such tremors as Fanny Burney experienced at the thought of her identity becoming known. She wrote without the stimulus of intercourse with literary men and celebrities and she had no need of their patronage after her books were written: she wrote without need and without any extraordinary circumstance to force her into

[46] Jane Austen, *Northanger Abbey*. 1909. (ed. Dobson.) p. 25.

publicity. When we consider the turbulent lives of the earlier women writers, Aphra Behn's voyages across the Atlantic, M^rs^ Manley's desertion by her husband in London, Charlotte Lennox's adventurous youth in America, the quiet existence which Jane Austen led at Steventon strikes us as the more remarkable. Perhaps there was need of some unusual spur to prick on the first women writers to their unusual calling. They had opposition to face which existed no longer in Jane Austen's time: she was held back neither by family objections nor by public opinion. She was able to face the fact of her authorship naturally and calmly, and free, in her own line, to reach perfection.

If we read Mary Wollstonecraft, whose *Vindication of the Rights of Women* had been published in 1792, we are apt to imagine that the position of women was worse than it was. The writer was of course a controversialist and anxious to make as much of her case as possible. She was, moreover, an unusual type of woman, who claimed more for her sex than the majority would have wished to claim for themselves. The women of culture and education of her own time, who might have been her best arguments in pleading the equality of reason and intellect between women and men, generally disapproved of the book. "I am sure I have as much liberty as I can make use of," said Hannah More,[47] and she was speaking for the greater part of her sex. It would be idle to pretend that Mary Wollstonecraft was not justified in her grounds of argument—even today we have not reached a state of equality of the sex such as she depicted—but when we remember that she lived in the society of Johnson's time, her attack seems unnecessarily violent. Had she looked back over the century which had passed since her fellow feminist Mary Astell wrote, she must have seen a steady improvement in the position of women. Perhaps she did see it and perhaps it was this record of the achievements of women during the eighteenth century that made her sex seem better worth the vindicating.

[47] Horace Walpole, *Letters.* XV, p. 337 and Hannah More, *Memoirs.* I, pp. 418–419. In this correspondence Mary Wollstonecraft is discussed, and the tone of it may be gathered from the fact that Walpole calls her a "hyena in petticoats" and Hannah More exclaims "from Liberty, Equality and the Rights of Man, good Lord deliver us."

# PART II

## "THE QUALITIES OF FEMALES"

### INTRODUCTION

We have followed the history of the novel as an element in the emancipation of women and seen the change in position of the woman author from Aphra Behn to Jane Austen. The eighteenth century is a century of change in the status not only of the woman writer but of the novel. Women came to the fore as authors and the novel developed: the novel developed and women came to the fore as authors. The novel is the one form of literature at the birth of which women have assisted. Poetry and drama existed before the woman poet and the woman dramatist; yet it is hardly too much to say that up to the present day there has been no woman poet or dramatist of the first rank. But there have been women novelists ever since the novel—in the accepted modern sense of the word—existed; and in the novel, women have indeed achieved the first rank. Surely it is no accident that brought about the connection of women with the novel, nor can we dismiss the question with a vague reference to changes in education and public opinion. We have to discover whether women have any special qualifications that fit them for this kind of writing and whether there is anything in their contribution to the novel which only women could have given.

Ever since man began to generalize at all, he has generalized about women. The "very woman," the type of femininity, exists in all literatures throughout the ages. Women, no doubt, have generalized about men; but until modern times, they have left no record of their conclusions. The Idea of Woman was a tradition so firmly established before women had the chance to retort, that they have not been able so successfully to evolve a "very man" to match her. We are biased by the opinion of centuries before we begin to look for signs of femininity. The eighteenth century accepted the traditional female mind, but did not accept its existence blindly. Having outgrown the stage when they debated whether woman had a soul or not, they now debated about her mind. On the whole, they did not doubt that the mind of woman was different in kind from that of man. In spite of occasional voices raised in prostest, from Mary Astell to Mary Wollstonecraft, who laid the blame for woman's inferiority on education, background, training—all that we may call by the name of the feminine tradition—the majority firmly believed that "the sex" was inferior by Nature. There is a conversation in *Sir Charles Grandison*[1] which is worth quoting as summing up the prevailing opinion. Old M^rs^ Shirley speaks on behalf of her sex:

"I think," said the venerable lady, "women are generally too much considered as a species apart. . . . . In common intercourse and conversation, why are we to be perpetually considering the *sex* of the person we are talking to? Why must women always be addressed in an appropriated language; and not treated on the common footing of reasonable creatures?". . . . .

"But pray, Sir Charles," said M^rs^ Selby, "let me ask your opinion: Do you think that if women had the same opportunities, the same education, as men, they would not equal them in their attainments?"

"Women, my dear M^rs^ Selby, are women sooner than men are men" (replies Sir Charles). "They have not, therefore, generally, the learning time, that men have, if they had equal geniuses". . . .

"But let me ask you" (says Lady G.). "Do you think there is a natural inferiority in the faculties of the one sex? A natural superiority, in those of the other?". . . . .

"Generally speaking" (says Sir Charles) "I have no doubt but there is. . . . . Generally speaking, Charlotte. Not individually *you* ladies and *us* men: I believe all we who are present shall be ready to subscribe to your superiority, ladies. . . . . There is a difference, pardon me, ladies, we are speaking *generally*, in the *constitution*, in the *temperament*, of the two sexes, that gives to one the advantage which it denies to the other. . . . . Why has nature made a difference in the beauty, proportion and symmetry, in the *persons* of the two sexes? Why gave it delicacy, softness, grace, to that of the women—as in the ladies before me: strength, firmness, to men. . . . . Weaker powers are given generally for weaker purposes in the economy of Providence. I, for my part, however, disapprove not of our venerable M^rs^ Shirley's observation; that we are apt to consider the sex *too much* as a species apart; yet it is my

[1] Richardson, *Sir Charles Grandison*. London, 1883. IV, p. 205 etc. (*Works*. Vol. XII.)

opinion that both God and nature have designed a very apparent difference in the minds of both, as well as in the peculiar beauties of their persons. . . . . Supposing, my Charlotte, that all human souls are in themselves, equal; yet the very design of the different machines in which they are enclosed, is to superinduce a temporary difference in their original equality; a difference adapted to the different purposes for which they are designed by Providence in the present transitory state. When these purposes are at an end, this difference will be at an end too. When sex ceases, inequality of souls will cease; and women will certainly be on a foot with men, as to intellectuals, in Heaven."

Neither the tone of gallantry in which Sir Charles conducts his arguments, nor the arguments themselves, calling to God, Nature, and Providence to support them, are calculated to convince or conciliate his female readers. But Richardson, as we have seen, was a feminist up to a point, and he did not come to such conclusions without thought. Also, in ascribing inferiority of mind to women, he does not regard them merely as a weaker copy of the men. In what he calls their "softness, delicacy, grace," he sees virtues which are denied to the male part of the species. Throughout *Clarissa* and *Sir Charles Grandison*, he is feeling after the differences in male and female psychology and, here and there, he makes a discovery that bears on the question of the woman writer. Believing what he did, it is interesting to see his opinion of the contribution women were capable of making to literature.

One question which Richardson raises is that of a feminine style. He speaks through the mouth of Clarissa: "Who sees not," would she say,[2] "that those women who take delight in writing, excel the men in all the graces of the familiar style. The gentleness of their minds, the delicacy of their sentiments (improved by the manner of their education) and the liveliness of their imaginations, qualify them to a high degree of preferences for this employment, while men of learning as they are called (that is to say men of *mere* learning), aiming to get above that natural ease and freedom which distinguish this, (and indeed every other kind of writing) when they think they have best succeeded are not above, or rather beneath, all natural beauty." The familiar style, says Richardson, is the province of women—the style of the letter, the diary and,

[2] Richardson, *Clarissa.* V, p. 459. (*Works.* Vol. VIII.)

indeed, of the novel—and the familiar style was born in literature just about the time when women began to write. "This I am resolved to write in a plain natural style," says Margaret, Duchess of Newcastle, in the Preface to her *Life of the Duke*,[3] "without Latin sentences, moral instructions, politic designs, feigned orations or envious and malicious exclamations." She is, unconsciously, defining the new prose as distinct from the old—is she at the same time defining the feminine style? Whether we restrict the style of women to the plain and familiar or not, we have to admit that we cannot imagine them writing the old ornate prose of the early seventeenth century.

There is more, however, in this prose than "Latin sentences." Bound up with the classics as it was, more than learning went to its making. It is a matter of words and rhythms, and, on the whole, (for like Sir Charles we must be careful to speak *generally*) women have never equalled men in the management of these. They have never shown the same power or the same delight in playing with words. This is a sweeping generalization but there are some facts to support it. One is the rarity of the great woman poet. Poetry is a thing of the intuition, and women are popularly supposed to be creatures of intuition, yet, in poetry, they have rarely reached the heights. Where they have written best, their greatness is often in the feeling of the poem rather than in the intoxicating quality of mere words. Another fact which may be adduced to support our argument is the comparatively small vocabulary of most women in ordinary conversations. The average man uses many more words than the woman who is his equal in education. The woman knows and recognizes the same words, but she does not use them; out of the several hundreds of epithets, which she understands in reading, she is often content with a score of the most popular for the needs of everyday intercourse. All this may be beside the point, yet it seems to bear on the question of the rise of the woman novelist. We cannot conceive of a woman who could write the prose of Sir Thomas Browne's *Urn Burial* any more than we can believe that the first chorus in Swinburne's *Atalanta* could have been written by a woman. But when a prose literature in the familiar style developed, women began to write with success. Surely this is more than a mere coincidence.

[3] Margaret, Duchess of Newcastle, *Life of William Cavendish*. London, 1886. (ed. C. H. Firth.) Preface.

It is Clarissa who starts us on another train of thought with regard to differences between the sexes, when she says that "wit with men was one thing: with women another"[4] and quotes Cowley to support her statement.

> 'Tis not a tale, 'tis not a jest
> Admired with laughter at a feast . . . .
> Much less can that have any place
> At which a virgin hides her face.

In applying what Cowley wrote of true wit in general to female wit in particular, Richardson again shows himself a subtle observer of feminine psychology—for these lines say truly what a woman's sense of humour is *not.* It is not rich in anecdote; everyone must have observed that it is men who are the chief sinners in this applied form of humour, as they must also have the credit for the occasions when they make apt use of other people's stories. It is not, either, of the type to be "admired with laughter at a feast," the humour which arises in conviviality of which Shakespeare and Fielding are masters. It is not of the kind "at which a virgin hides her face," a kind which women rarely originate and into which they do not readily enter. When a woman becomes coarse she is revolting while a man may still be amusing, and this is one of the reasons why women could not write with success for the Elizabethan or the Restoration stage. The spirit of comedy in those days demanded something broader and coarser than most women are capable of giving. Aphra Behn, who had led a man's life and who was besides a woman of unusual liveliness and vigour, managed to enter into this spirit, but for most women it was impossible. Comedy in those days demanded, moreover, a special form of verbal wit, compounded of puns, plays on words, and glorified abuse—another manner of speech which has never sat easily on women. It is the male comedian today who is the most unblushing punster; it is the schoolboy and not his sister who rivals the comic characters of Shakespeare in his mastery of the joyous art of finding uncomplimentary names for friends and enemies. One can only suggest that the humour of women is "measurable" like their temperament. There are some works, some characters which it is impossible to think of as the creation of a woman. Samuel Butler may have enjoyed creating a sensation in advancing his theory that the Homeric poems are the work of a woman, but no one has ever let

[4] *Clarissa.* III, p. 258. (*Works.* Vol. VI.)

fancy run away with him enough to suggest that Shakespeare was a woman. Falstaff is the great example, of course, of the humorous character who never could have been conceived by a woman: it is generally claimed, indeed, that no women can even appreciate Falstaff, and this is probably true to the extent that few women would want to meet Falstaff in the flesh. But there are lesser humourists, also, whose works, it seems to me, a woman would never have written—W. S. Gilbert, for instance, or Edward Lear. Farce and nonsense are not the fields for women's humour: at her best a woman is still "captive to the truth of a foolish world" and does not create and people a world of her own. But while we may allow that a woman could not have written *Henry IV* or the *Nonsense Rhymes*, we must admit at the same time that the finest touches of Jane Austen's humour could not have been achieved by a man. Once again, however, we are generalizing.

A final point is suggested by Richardson in the words "Women are women sooner than men are men." Educationalists and psychologists agree that woman matures earlier than man, not intellectually so much as emotionally. She is "grown up" at an earlier age. This fact shows that in some things sex is stronger than education, and it may be of importance in the study of the woman writer. D^r Johnson said of *Evelina* that he did not know of any man who could write as good a book so young, and it is a fact worth noting that many women novelists produce their best books at an early age. Fanny Burney never again wrote anything so good as *Evelina*, and in other cases, also, one finds that wider experience of the world deadens rather than stimulates the first impulse to write.

Perhaps "women are women sooner than men are men," too, in the sense that they are more inevitably governed by their sex. Tradition which calls them "the sex" as though women alone had sex, certainly suggests that this is so. But we must not generalize before examining their works, and even then we can only speak with reservations. The women novelists of the eighteenth century are only a small group and anything we can say about them must surely have an exception somewhere. The above suggestions are the merest theorizing, taking up an eighteenth century point of view and showing that, in essentials, it is a possible one today. And, perhaps, even in the end we shall not get beyond points of view and theorizing. Even if, after an examination of the works of a number of women novelists, we find differences from the male novelist that can only be ascribed to difference in sex, we may be still as far from proving the existence of a feminine mind as ever. But if facts which seem to indicate a feminine mind really point only to a mind governed by a feminine tradition, perhaps the feminine tradition itself is worth the study.

## CHAPTER I

## THE BEGINNINGS OF THE PSYCHOLOGICAL NOVEL

### 1. Autobiography and Letters

In one of M^r^ Aldous Huxley's novels, *Crome Yellow*, there is a conversation which is an amusing criticism of a certain kind of novel very common at the present day. Dennis Stone, a young writer, has confessed that he is writing a novel.

"Of course," (says M^r^ Scogan, an older member of the party) "I'll describe the plot for you. Little Percy, the hero, was never good at games but he was always clever. He passes through the usual public school and the usual university and comes to London, where he lives among the artists. He is bowed down with melancholy thought; he carries the whole weight of the Universe upon his shoulders. He writes a novel of dazzling brilliance; he dabbles delicately in Amour and disappears at the end of the book into the luminous future."[1] At this point, Dennis blushes and secretly resolves to tear up the manuscript so accurately and mercilessly described. At this point, too, perhaps, the reader may blush and think of the manuscript he had hoped to give to the world or the novel he had it in his heart to write. No one can fail to recognize the type of novel implied. It is no unjust account of half the novels published in England every year. It is, indeed, the sort of novel we have come to expect, the sort which the mediocre novelist finds easiest to write. Often such a novel is pure autobiography, for the young writer readily takes to himself the advice of Sidney's Muse to "look in his heart and write." He is encouraged to do so by the whole trend of modern education, which takes "self-expression" for its slogan and encourages the child, from its earliest years, to record its commonplace thoughts as though they were epoch-making. He is encouraged, too, by the flood of autobiographical literature, memoirs, diaries, and reminiscences which

[1] Aldous Huxley, *Crome Yellow*. New York, 1922. p. 30.

issues every year from the press. We call his novel "psychological" and speak of the "reactions" of the characters to the circumstances of the story: such is the jargon of the day. They did not use these words in the eighteenth century, but it was then that the type of novel to which they are applied began. From the objectivity of the old romances and the hundred merry tales of the jest books, the modern novel emerged. It is Richardson who is generally given the credit for the change and most of it he deserves, for *Pamela* was the first novel consciously approached from the subjective point of view. But the novel does not suddenly become subjective and "psychological," and, for its beginnings we must look further back than *Pamela.*

It is a far cry from the "best-seller" of modern times to the romances that Dorothy Osborne read, and we must look for the beginnings of the change, not in the novel as it was in the seventeenth century, but in the letters, memoirs, and diaries of the period. The old romance was purely objective. It is safe to say that no modern reader ever lost himself in the *Grand Cyrus* or *Clelia.* Their characteristics are probably better known through the parodies written upon them than from the texts themselves. One sympathizes with Glanville, in the *Female Quixote,* who could not read through *Cassandra,* even though his refusal cost him the love of the romantic Arabella. To enter upon one of these stories is to enter an impenetrable forest where one is lost in bypaths and forgets even where one was going, where there are clearings but never, it seems, an end. Even the people one meets by the way are not men of like passions with ourselves. They have a language of their own and rule their lives by a special code of honour.

One wonders, indeed, how these endless stories could ever have kept Dorothy Osborne on tenterhooks for the next volume or M^rs^ Pepys from her night's rest. They must have accepted, to begin with, the fact that the world of fiction was not the world of real life. For while Dorothy was devoting her leisure hours to the Scudérys and La Calprenède, she was herself writing, in her letters to Sir William Temple, a real love story for posterity to read. It seems curious to us that she could have argued gravely on the merits of the cases of the four lovers[2] in the *Grand Cyrus* without realizing the artificiality of their passions, she who could write

[2] Dorothy Osborne, *Letters.* New York, 1888. (ed. Parry.) Letter 32, p. 154.

of her own feelings with such delicacy and truth. The reader, who never enters for a moment into the emotions of Statira, feels with Dorothy in her anxiety for her letters or in her joy when she receives them. A letter from Sir William arrives in the midst of a card game. "In the midst of our play in comes my blessed boy with your letter and, in earnest, I was not able to disguise the joy it gave me, though one was by that is not much your friend and took notice of a blush that for my life I could not keep back. I put up the letter in my pocket and made what haste I could to lose the money I had left, that I might take occasion to go fetch some more but I did not make such haste back again—."[3]

An insensible groom who is the bearer of another letter will look after his horse while he keeps her in suspense. "I could not imagine him so very a beast as to think his horses were to be served before me and therefore was presently struck with an apprehension he had no letter for me: it went cold to my heart as ice, and hardly left me courage enough to ask him the question: but when he drawled it out, that he thought there was a letter for me in his bag, I quickly made him leave his broom. 'Twas well 'tis a dull fellow, he could not but have discerned else that I was strangely overjoyed with it and earnest to have it; for, though the poor fellow made what haste he could to untie his bag, I did nothing but chide him for being so slow. Last I had it, and in earnest I know not whether an entire diamond of the bigness on 't would have pleased me half so well."[4]

These are the little incidents which make up the love stories of every age. And how unconvincing are the set speeches of the lovers in the pages of the Scudérys, beside Dorothy Osborne's tender naïve avowals—reserved enough in the earlier letters and only taking courage as the courtship progresses to admit that "I have such a habit of thinking of you, that every other thought intrudes and proves uneasy to me,"[5] or "Love is a terrible word and I should blush to death if anything but a letter accused me on 't."[6] Sometimes there is a note of tragedy in the letters, when the lovers have quarrelled and Dorothy is beset with difficulties in her home life. She tries to convince herself that love is a fond passion while

[3] *Ibid.*, Letter 10, p. 68.

[4] *Ibid.*, Letter 13, p. 79.

[5] *Ibid.*, Letter 10, p. 69.

[6] *Ibid.*, Letter 31, p. 151.

she still has one eye out of the window, looking for the carrier's cart. Like Fanny Greville, she prays for indifference—"from this hour, we'll live quietly, no more fears, no more jealousies."[7] But her affairs, mercifully, right themselves and the reader is gratified with a happy ending.

Dorothy wrote without art in a style "free and easy as one's discourse, not studied as an oration, nor made up of hard words like a charm."[8] She thinks it not unworthy to record the trivial events of her everyday life. With her good wishes to her lover she sends a prosaic remedy for his cold. She writes of love—and quince marmalade. As a result, we can enter into her changes of mood as into those of the heroines of the modern psycho-analytical age. "Can there be a romancer story than ours?"[9] she writes in 1654, with her marriage now in sight. Yet she still looked for her romance in her French tomes—they took her out of Chicksands and its monotony as they took M^rs^ Pepys out of the loneliness of Axe Yard. I have quoted at length from her letters because she seems to me to bring home the contrast between objectivity of the artificial romances that were her form of fiction, and the more subjective quality of the story of real life, which was to be the foundation of the modern novel. But it is only by accident that we have her letters and she had no thought of posterity when she wrote them. With the Autobiography of the Duchess of Newcastle, it is a different matter.

That "Mad Madge of Newcastle," well known to her age as an eccentric, "a raree-show in her own person," should write her own life, was probably regarded by her contemporaries as only another of her vagaries. For us, however, it has an interest above her philosophical poems and fancies, in some ways even above the *Life of the Duke*—for it was the first work of its kind to be published in England. The Englishman is not, by nature, an autobiographical animal. The English Renaissance had produced no Cardan, no Cellini, no Montaigne. Sir Thomas Browne, preoccupied with the "humour of his irregular self," exploring the microcosm to discover more of the microcosm, is an early instance of the student of self, but, even then, no one would pretend that *Religio Medici* was pure autobiography. There had been other

[7] *Ibid.*, Letter 47, p. 214.
[8] *Ibid.*, Letter 33, p. 160.
[9] *Ibid.*, Letter 48, p. 218.

lives also—Thomas Tusser's and Thomas Bodley's, for instance, which were written by the authors about themselves; but, in these, the stress is on events rather than on the character of the writers. Lord Herbert's life stands between these and the life of the Duchess. It is subjective but it had the excuse also of being a record of a period of great political interest. The Duchess had no such excuse. She wrote to please herself and to satisfy a conviction of her own that she was interesting enough to write about. It is for the author's avowed purpose in writing that the *True Relation of my Birth, Breeding and Life* is a new departure in English literature. And, interesting from the point of view of this study, is the fact that its author is a woman.

The impulse to confession, as a motive for literature, is rarely found before the seventeenth century, in England at least. Towards the end of the seventeenth century and from that time onward, there is a good deal of it. While it is true enough that the habit of introspection is a matter of the individual temperament, at any time, and we say that one person is introspective and another is not, it is also true that there is a common temperament which is formed by the current thought of the age. Today it is the fashion to be introspective, with the result that an extreme love of self-study is developed in those whose natural bias is toward it, and that a tendency towards introspection is discernible even in the most objective—say a typical Rugby footballer. As far as this is true we can say that the sixteenth century was objective and the seventeenth was not. It is a matter for speculation why the change came about just at that time. The new interest in the subjective may have a connection with new movements in philosophy. It may well be that Descartes, starting with the ego, as a basis for his philosophical system, stimulated an interest in the self in humbler minds, incapable of grasping entire the Cartesian philosophy. Great scientific and philosophical movements generally have their popular counterpart and if there is, indeed, a connection between the method of Descartes and the new subjectivity in literature, the Duchess is a happy illustration. She had belonged to the circle in Paris in which the Duke conversed with Descartes and Hobbes, then in the full tide of the discussion which followed upon the publication of Descartes's works; and though she "never spoke to Master Hobbes twenty words in her life" and could not speak even one word to Descartes in his own language, she had opportunities of hearing their conversation and of gaining from it some impressions. Perhaps, however, Descartes's philosophy is an instance of a general tendency, of something that was "in the air" and the Duchess was only expressing the same thing in literature.

Whether inspired by the age, or merely by the whim of an individual, the Duchess's *True Relation* is a pattern of all the autobiography ever written. She allows her faults as to a confessor: her ambition—"I repine not at the gifts that Nature or Fortune bestows upon others, yet I am a great emulator: for though I wish none worse than they are, yet it is lawful for me to wish myself the best, and to do my honest endeavour thereunto. For I think it no crime to wish myself the exactest of Nature's works, my thread of life the longest, my chain of destiny the strongest, my mind the peaceablest, my life the pleasantest, my death the easiest, and the greatest saint in Heaven";[10] her womanish cowardice—"I am the veriest coward in nature, as upon the sea or any dangerous places, or of thieves or fire or the like. Nay the shooting of a gun although but a pot-gun will make me start . . . .."[11] She shows subtlety in the study of her own temperament, in noting the strange melancholy reserve that makes her love "though extraordinarily and constantly yet not fondly but soberly and observingly."[12] She is pathetically conscious of her own self-consciousness, which made her a failure at Court—"I was so bashful when I was out of my mother's, brothers' and sisters' sight, whose presence used to give me confidence."[13] Throughout the whole runs the persuasion that she is "different," the starting point of all autobiographies—and, moreover, a pride in the fact that she is different. What she says of her clothes is typical of her attitude to the rest of life. "I took great delight in attiring, fine dressing and fashion, especially such fashions as I did invent myself, not taking that pleasure in such fashions as was invented by others. Also, I did dislike any should follow my fashions, for I always took delight in a singularity even in accoutrements of habits."[14] Finally she sets forth her purpose in writing.

[10] Margaret, Duchess of Newcastle, *The True Relation of My Birth, Breeding and Life*. London, 1886. (ed. C. H. Firth.) p. 315.

[11] *Ibid.*, p. 317.

[12] *Ibid.*, p. 313.

[13] *Ibid.*, p. 286.

[14] *Ibid.*, p. 312.

"Neither did I intend this piece to delight but to divulge, not to please the fancy but to tell the truth, lest after ages should mistake in not knowing I was daughter to one Master Lucas of St. John's, near Colchester in Essex, Second wife to the Lord Marquis of Newcastle: for my Lord having had two wives, I might easily have been mistaken, especially if I should die and my Lord marry again."[15] It would have seemed a hard fate for the Duchess, to have been confused with the first or hypothetical third wife of the Duke, though, had she known, she was in no danger of it. The anxiety to preserve her identity, to keep herself alive when her body is dead, recalls the words of Montaigne in his foreword from the author to the reader, where he dedicates his "well-meaning Booke"[16] to his kinsfolk and friends "to the end that, losing me (which they are likely to do ere long) they may therein find some lineaments of my conditions and humours and, by that means, reserve more whole and more lively foster, the knowledge and acquaintance they have had of me." In this final paragraph of the life of the Duchess, we see more than a desire for self-expression—it is self-advertisement. Like the Countess of Oxford and Asquith, she says in effect "Here's me."[17]

There must be many interesting letters and diaries and perhaps autobiographies of the period which have not come down to us. There remain enough to show that the fashion of keeping personal records and private memoirs was growing. The religious struggles of the times produced a crop of their own and Quakerism in particular has made a contribution to this kind of literature. Among such works, leaving out of account all purely domestic records, such as the *Diary* of Lady Anne Clifford, who kept her Journal in the same spirit as she kept her household accounts, we must notice, in particular, two autobiographies by women. One of these—Lucy Hutchinson's—is a mere fragment prefixed to her life of Colonel Hutchinson. It was written, probably, about the same time as the Duchess's, but it was not written for publication. M[rs] Hutchinson wrote her own life and her husband's, first for the benefit of her children, to "stir up thankfulness for things past" and to illustrate the Providence of God. Her moral purpose is the mainspring of her narrative, and yet, for a moment, she

[15] *Ibid.*, p. 318.
[16] Montaigne, *Essays*. (trans. Florio.) London, 1898. I. Preface.
[17] Margor Asquith, *Autobiography*. I, p. 51.

becomes interested in herself and gives us an account which is all too brief, of how she too was different from the rest of the world in her youth. But the page is torn where she tries to write down her early sins as though she shrank from recording, even to herself, such intimate particulars of her life. M^rs Hutchinson is no dispassionate self-student, like the Duchess, though she is interesting as another instance of a sign of the times. Nor did Ann Fanshawe write her own *Memoirs* in the same spirit as her Grace of Newcastle. Having lived through the turbulent times of the Civil War, she addressed to her son an account of the "most remarkable actions and accidents of your family . . . . I would not have you a stranger to it, because, by the example, you may imitate what is applicable to your condition in the world, and endeavour to avoid those misfortunes we have passed through, if God pleases."[18] Like Lucy Hutchinson, Lady Fanshawe tells us too little about herself, except indirectly, in the accounts of how she conducted herself in her many dangers and difficulties. But it is something that these ladies found it worth while to write at all. The fact, also, that they wrote of their husbands is significant. We feel the pride of possession in the accounts of Sir Richard Fanshawe, Colonel Hutchinson, and in the Duchess's uncritical praise of "my lord." All these ladies had adventurous lives which shook them out of themselves and it may have been due to this that they compiled their family records. Whatever the reason, in their accounts we have something that is nearer to the modern novel than the form of fiction which went by the name of novel at the time when they were written. In the Duchess of Newcastle, especially, we approach the modern spirit, for she not only wrote her life, but published it.

## 2. The Novel before "Pamela"

The Duchess of Newcastle was an amateur. She could write a romance like the *Blazing World*, "romancical, philosophical, fantastical," and it was all one to her if the public read it or laughed at it. Aphra Behn, on the other hand, was a professional writer, faced with the necessity of supporting herself. When, after a career of failure and success as a playwright, she took to novel-writing, it was solely with an eye to giving the public what it wanted. This is no place to discuss the state of the novel when

[18] Lady Ann Fanshawe, *Memoirs*. 1907. p. 1.

Aphra Behn began to write. It is enough to say that there were two forms of popular fiction—the long romance whose reign had been inaugurated at the beginning of the century by d'Urfé's *Astrée* and of which Roger Boyle's *Parthenissa*, published in 1656, is perhaps the best-known English example; and the short tale or "novella," the lineal descendant of the collections of narratives and jest books of the Middle Ages. The characteristics of the romances have already been sketched—these, for their "unparalleled purity" and elevated sentiments were the reading of the upper classes of society. The novel was a more popular form of fiction. The Italian "novella" on which it was based was short, realistic, and domestic. "Novels are of a more familiar nature," says Congreve in the preface to his *Incognita*, "come near to us and represent to us intrigues in practice, delight us with accidents and odd events but not such as are wholly unusual or unprecedented: such as not being so distant from our belief, bring also the pleasure nearer us. Romances give more wonder, novels more delight." One cannot, however, generalize so easily about the novel as about the romance. "Novel" was a useful word, applicable to any tale which was short enough. It might be a high-toned tale of love, like Boccaccio's story of the falcon, or a racy story of low life like Deloney's *Jack of Newberie*; it was a vehicle alike of tender sentiment or bawdy humour. But whatever its material, it was a straight-told tale. The story was the thing, and the characters mere agents in the intrigue.

It is not surprising that Aphra Behn chose to write novels. It was a form of fiction easily turned out. It required little invention, an old theme newly set being as good as a new one to most people. It was capable of many variations—a means of gratifying the taste of the age for licentiousness, as well as for wonder and romance. Aphra Behn's novels fall into two groups—serious love stories, generally tragic, the scenes of which are laid in France, Holland, Spain, or Italy and the more familiar, domestic narratives of English life. The first written, though not the first published, were of the latter kind, written no doubt while she was still in the midst of her career as a dramatist and influenced by the comedy spirit. *The Little Black Lady*, her earliest attempt at fiction, *The King of Bantam*, *The Unfortunate Happy Lady*, and probably *The Unfortunate Bride*, *The Wandering Beauty*, and *The Unhappy Mistake* all belong to the period between 1680 and 1687. Of these *The Little Black Lady*, *The King of Bantam* and *The Unfortunate Bride* are practically worthless. In the first, especially, the author has not even the interest to name her characters, and the ending is purely the device of a jest book. They are written in an early colloquial style, they give us occasional glimpses of the manners of the period, but, in the history of the novel, they are nothing. *The Unfortunate Happy Lady*, *The Wandering Beauty*, and *The Unhappy Mistake* are better, in that they are livelier and less carelessly worked out. They contain some interesting pictures of English life—the cottage and country house in *The Wandering Beauty*, the tale of a beautiful serving-maid who married a lord half a century before *Pamela*; or the scenes in Tower Yard in *The Unhappy Mistake*—with its picturesque beef-eaters and the watchman crying a starlit morning. To my mind, they are better—certainly pleasanter—stories than her tragedies of intrigue, but to the student of the psychological novel their value is less. The characters are but types whose names are forgotten as soon as read. Who, indeed, can remember whether Philadelphia was the Unfortunate Bride or the Unfortunate Happy Lady?

The novel by which M^rs^ Behn's name is known even to those who have not read her is *Oroonoko*, first published in 1688. It stands apart from the others not only by reason of its greater length but because it was remarkable as a new type of story. It may still be read with pleasure even by the reader who is not a student of literature. It had its foundation in a true experience of the author's. She protests in the first paragraph that it is no "feigned hero" of whom she writes and that she had heard his story from his own mouth. Yet Oroonoko is given all the qualities of the hero of romance. The racial features of the negro are altered to make him beautiful according to European standards. "His nose was rising and Roman instead of African and flat: his mouth the finest shaped that could be seen: far from those great turn'd lips that are so natural to the rest of the negroes. The whole proportion and air of his face was so nobly and exactly form'd, that bating his colour, there could be nothing in Nature more beautiful agreable and handsome."[19] More than that, he has had a European education and in his native country of Coramantien has managed to acquire a knowledge of Morals, Language, Science, and the man-

[19] Aphra Behn, *Works*. 1915. (ed Summers.) V, p. 136.

ners of an English gentleman. He makes love like an Elizabethan sonneteer, and, swearing his faith to the "Black Venus," Imoinda, vows he will have "an eternal Idea in his mind of the charms she now wore: and should look into his Heart for that Idea when he could find it no longer in her face."[20] Though he is a great warrior and slayer of wild beasts, he languishes, sighs, grows pensive, swoons at the sight of Imoinda. As a picturesque figure his success in undoubted; as a negro Prince actually in slavery in Surinam, he is harder to believe in. In spite of the assertions of the eyewitness, Mrs Behn, one never feels, indeed, that Oroonoko and Imoinda are people in real life. But there is another and more real figure who plays a part in these scenes of tropical life, and that is Aphra Behn herself. Not only did she hit on the idea of turning her own experience to account in fiction, but she could not keep herself out of her story. It is not merely to give vividness to her story that she introduces herself. She is anxious also to let her readers know that she is Aphra Behn, who has seen all these wonders that they have not. She likes us to know that she lived in the best house in Surinam, that she played on the flute to the natives, that it was she who brought home and presented to the King's Theatre the feathered native dress worn in the *Indian Queen*. In the midst of the description of an Indian village, she stops to tell us that "at the time my own hair was cut short and I had a Taffety cap with black feathers on my head."[21] This is the same Mrs Behn who liked to mix herself up in the affairs of nations and to manage her diplomatic missions by setting Dutchmen "on a blaze."

The rest of her novels are all of a piece and by no means reach the standard of *Oroonoko*, but they have their points of interest. They have the same confusing titles as the comedies—*The Fair Jilt*, *Agnes de Castro*, and *The Nun*, published in 1688; *The Lucky Mistake* and a second *Nun* in 1689; and *The Dumb Virgin*, published posthumously. As stories they are full of the intrigues, "accidents and odd events," which Congreve notes as characteristic of the novel, but we cannot go further with him and say that these events are "not wholly unusual or unprecedented." They reflect a state of society in which events are as surprising and fortuitous as in the romances, only quickened up to succeed each other at a more rapid pace. There are duels, murders, elopements,

[20] *Ibid.*, p. 139.
[21] *Ibid.*, p. 185.

rapes—a host of unnatural and unnecessary crimes. *The Nun, or the Perjur'd Beauty* called "a true novel," beginning with a street fight so confused that one can hardly distinguish the combatants, ends, like an Elizabethan tragedy, with the violent death of all the characters save one, who dies twenty-four hours later "with all the happy symptoms of a departing saint."[22] Yet these stories, incredible as they may seem, are supposedly tales of modern life, only laid abroad, where they might pass for truth on the ground that *omni ignotum est pro magnifico*. Perhaps, if we are to trust contemporary opinion, the convents where the nuns plot elopements and conduct amorous intrigues are not so far removed from the real life of the day as they seem. At any rate in the Dutch scenes, which are the background to *The Fair Jilt* and *The Fair Vow-breaker*, M[rs] Behn is writing of what she knew and we come across a little domestic picture such as Isabella's washing-day, which strikes us oddly in the midst of so many improbabilities. It is as if, while taking over the conventions of the novel of intrigue, ready made, the author could not forbear to introduce touches of actual life.

One does not expect to find psychological truth in the characters of these novels; yet one or two points of interest emerge. There is one character which we meet in almost every story—and that is the aggressive woman. It is always a woman who is the spring of the action. The men are mere puppets with very little of the hero in them. Even Dangerfield in *The Dumb Virgin*, who is as fine an English gentleman as Aphra ever saw step in the Mall, is little more than a low adventurer. But the women are leaders in crime and leaders in love. They do not observe the condition which Jane Austen quotes in *Northanger Abbey* "that no young lady can be justified in falling in love before the gentleman's love is declared."[23] But then Aphra Behn was no "young lady," nor were her characters. There is Isabella—the nun and fair vow-breaker who avows her love through a convent grille, persuades her lover to elope with her, and afterwards smothers him and sends a second husband to his death along with him. There is Elvira who strikes a harsh note in the mediaeval sweetness of *Agnes de Castro*. Best of all, there is Miranda, the fair jilt, who begins life as a *fille dévote*, makes love to a priest in the confessional,

[22] *Ibid.*, p. 348.
[23] Richardson, *Rambler*, p. 97.

and sees him languish for years in prison as a result, sends her page to the scaffold in an attempt engineered by herself to murder her sister (and would have caused the death of her husband in the same way had not the headsman blundered), and ends triumphantly penitent. The strength of the stories lies in the feelings of these women. Miranda is intolerable, but she has power. *The Fair Vow-breaker* is a bad story, but here and there, as if by accident, it is true to life; as when Isabella, thinking herself perfectly balanced and superior to the attractions of sex, meets Henault and realizes she is "as feeble a woman as the most unresolved."[24] In *The Lucky Mistake*, again, there is truth to life in the picture of Atlanta, a maiden nurtured on "delicate philosophy, fit for the study of ladies,"[25] who reasons gravely as to whether she should accept a letter from the youth by whom she is already prepossessed and finally answers it—to save her sister's credit! It is as if Mrs Behn, writing on a theme she knew, a woman in love, refused for a moment to be bound by convention and began to write what a woman would feel. Then, remembering she was writing, not of women, but of heroines, she slipped again into the old style and wrote dispassionately of the sighs and tears, the "raptures and excesses" of emotion.

Two works, published in successive years, are of especial interest in the period before *Pamela*—the *Adventures of Rivella* by Mrs Manley in 1714 and the story called *Bosvil and Galesia*, which is one of the collection of *Entertaining Novels* by Jane Barker, published in 1715. In both these novels we see autobiography becoming the stuff of fiction. Which of these two ladies first conceived the idea of making of her own life a tale for the public it is hard to say. *Rivella* was first in print, but it is very probable that *Bosvil and Galesia* was written many years before it was published. Its theme is the same as that of the "unkind Strephon" poems of 1688; and the material of a collection like the *Entertaining Novels* may have been many years in the making. Neither could anyone suspect a young lady of Jane Barker's academic circles following the lead of a woman of Mrs Manley's notoriety, even if *Rivella* ever penetrated into the innocent country life of Wilsthorp, near Stamford in Lincolnshire. It is safer to conclude

[24] Aphra Behn, *Works*. V, p. 277.

[25] *Ibid.*, p. 366. This, no doubt, refers to Fontenelle's *Pluralité des Mondes*.

that the idea occurred to two people about the same time and to both we must give the credit of being pioneers.

It is probable that the earliest readers of *Rivella* thought of it only as another volume in the history of contemporary scandal for which its author had made herself famous. In the words "Secret Memoirs" on the title-page lay its strongest appeal to the public in an age when even a critical reader like Lady Mary Wortley Montagu could regret that, by the arrest of the author for libel, future volumes of the *New Atlantis* were lost to the world.[26] Perhaps Mrs Manley only wrote of herself because, after her promise made before the Attorney-General to entertain her readers with "mere gentle pleasing themes" in future, it was a safer means of indulging her flair for scandal. Or perhaps Curll was speaking the truth when he said that Mrs Manley wrote her own life for fear someone else would write it first. But whatever her motive, no one can doubt that she enjoyed the writing of her own story. After the formlessness of the *Atlantis*, the crowding of many characters who change their names in every volume, the confusion of allegory, moralizing, and romance, it is a relief to turn to the one full-length portrait of Rivella. We should not join today in Lady Mary's lament for the lost volumes of *Atlantis;* we might indeed spare one of the volumes that we have, without too great a sense of loss. Court scandals have only a passing interest and the dashes, pseudonyms, and keys which, no doubt, made the work very "secret" indeed, and were part of its success, are only irritating when the need for concealment is past. But we are still interested to know what the author of the *New Atlantis* thought about herself.

Even in the *Atlantis* there are indications that Mrs Manley was her own favourite heroine, as the Duchess of Marlborough was her favourite villain. She drags her own affairs before the public both in the story of M. L'Ingrate in Book I, where her literary career is touched on, and in the account, in Book II, of her early life and marriage with Manley. But in *Rivella* she begins in the style of the true autobiographer with her childhood and takes us through her life, a triumphal progress of self-praise. By throwing the task of making her defense upon an imaginary Sir Charles Lovemore, who is asked by the young Chevalier D'Aumont to

[26] Lady Mary Wortley Montagu, *Letters*. (Everyman.) p. 4.

describe to him the author of the *Atlantis*, she manages to pronounce her own eulogy with a better grace. About her faults she is only half-hearted. They are not really faults at all. "Her virtues are her own, her vices occasioned by her misfortunes";[27] she has a little affectation but "it becomes her admirably well"; she is extravagant but that is only part of her generosity; and while she courageously admits her want of beauty, she implies a fascination which more than makes up for it. But even while she suppresses anything that might cast a shade on her character, she is only making clearer the sort of woman she was. In the account of her relations with Hilaria, in her unpleasant intrigue with Sir Peter Vainlove, even in the completely incomprehensible lawsuit in which she becomes involved with Lord Crafty and Lord Meanwell, one impression is clear: that of Rivella, wire-pulling and intriguing with all her woman's wiles, "managing" everybody with whom she comes in contact. Where her power over men is in question she omits nothing. The whole account of her trial is a beautiful piece of feminine diplomacy. The *New Atlantis*, she protested, "was written without intending particular reflections on characters. When this was not believed and the contrary urged home to her by several circumstances and likenesses, she said then it must be inspiration, because, *knowing her own innocence*, she could count it no other way: the secretary then replied upon her that inspiration used to be upon a good account and her writings were stark naught, she told him, *with an air full of penitence*, that might be true, but it was as true there were evil angels as well as good, so that nevertheless, what she had wrote might still be inspiration."[28] And here the helpless judge had to dismiss the case, probably with the cry of his century, "Oh! the sex, the sex." *Rivella* comes to an end with an outburst that is lyrical. "Allons, let us go my dear Lovemore,"[29] interrupted young D'Aumont. "Let us not lose a moment before we are acquainted with the only person of her sex that knows how to live and of whom we may say in relation to love, since she has so peculiar a genius for and has made such noble discoveries in that passion, that it would have been a fault in her not to be faulty." It is rather cruel to turn from this glowing picture to a passing reference in Swift's *Journal to*

[27] Mrs Manley, *Adventures of Rivella*. 1714.
[28] *Ibid.*
[29] *Ibid.*

*Stella.* "Poor M^rs^ Manley, the author, is very ill of a dropsy and a sore leg . . . . I am hardly sorry for her; she has very generous principles for one of her sort: and a great deal of good sense and invention. She is about forty, very homely and very fat."[30]

While she is at pains to vindicate her character to the world at large, M^rs^ Manley does not omit a special reminder to the literary critic. She points out, in passing, what, in her opinion, are her strong points as a writer—and these may be summed up as one—that she "treats well of love."[31] Her scenes of passion—this is her own comment—are "such a representation of Nature as to warm the coldest reader."[32] She goes further than that and accredits herself with a moral purpose which her warmest admirer never saw in her, in that by her treatment of love she raises "a high idea of the dignity of human kind and informs us that we have in our composition wherewith to taste sublime and transporting joys."[33] It is interesting, at least, that she was consciously writing from her own experience. She knew "how to live," she had a peculiar genius for love, and so she wrote about it. The scenes she cites as her masterpieces, the encounter of Jermyn and the Duchess of Cleveland in the bedchamber, or the corruption of Charlotte Howard by the Duke of Portland, both from Book I of the *Atlantis*, show, at once, her limitations. Her theme, like M^rs^ Haywood's, later, is always *Love in Excess*, and unless the reader likes his pictures for the thickness with which the colour is laid on, rather than for delicacy of drawing, he will not be transported by the truth to Nature which he has been promised. Her method in trying to get at truth to life is to hide nothing—with the result that what she would have called a representation of warm and living passion is often merely an offence against good taste. Yet she tried to draw from life, though she had not skill enough—while the authors of the old romances drew from an Idea, like those early Italian painters who could have thought it a sacrilege to take a woman for their Madonna. It is surely something that she made the attempt. And a woman of her knowledge of the world could not write voluminously, as she did, without recording something of her own observations. Here and there is a shrewd com-

[30] Swift, *Journal to Stella.* Jan. 28, 1711–12.

[31] *Rivella.*

[32] *Ibid.*

[33] *Ibid.*

ment, a touch of psychological truth which is almost lost in the general hotch potch of books like the *Atlantis*, *Zarah*, and *Rivella*. There is the episode, in Book I of the *Atlantis*, of M^me^ St. Amant, who loves the Baron de Mezarcy without knowing it, where, for once, the author shows a delicacy into which she may have been drawn for the moment by a situation reminiscent of that of the *Princesse de Clèves*. Here M^rs^ Manley shows her knowledge of her own sex, not only in the study of M^me^ St. Amant herself, but in observations by the way such as the following: "She was not accustomed to read books of gallantry: knew no more of love than what she got from operas and comedies, where, *unless a lady has been in love before*, she seldom makes application"[34] or "No woman ever dies of a distemper of the mind, when she can once come to cry it out."[35] In the coarser parts of her narratives, too, we come across excellent examples of the sort of spite which is generally supposed to be peculiarly feminine: in the story of Arethusa (Lady Manchester) and her jealousy of Felicia (Lady Sunderland), there is a long conversation which shows how well M^rs^ Manley was acquainted with the "cat" in women. No doubt she herself had had to suffer from this sort of felinity.

Without going so far as to agree with the Secretary who condemned her writings as "stark naught," we should say that M^rs^ Manley is greater for what she attempted than for what she achieved. She went further than M^rs^ Behn in deliberately drawing from real people and real incidents, but the results of her observation are ill assimilated. Overborne by her desire to give the public something to talk about, and innocent of method, she produced in the *Atlantis* and *Zarah* a jumble of romantic fiction and political and social satire which compares badly with a straightforward narrative like *Oroonoko*. *Rivella*, though not free from the disorder which we find in all her works, is given a unity by its central character and remains the most readable, as well as the most original, of her works.

The other autobiographical novel already referred to, *Bosvil and Galesia*, had a very different history from *Rivella*, as Jane Barker was a very different sort of woman from M^rs^ Manley. It was written not to defend the character of its author—for Miss Barker was a lady of unexceptionable character, in spite of her

[34] M^rs^ Manley, *New Atlantis*. London, 1709. I, p. 113.
[35] *Ibid*., I, p. 120.

knowledge of Latin and her study of "Harvey his circulatio sanguinis"—but to ease her heart. "Writing, in this my lonely state, was like discoursing or disburthening ones heart to a friend."[35a] Thus much she discovered for herself. It is probable that this was not the earliest version of her unhappy love affair. In her first discovery that Bosvil was faithless, she tells us how she thought of suicide, but changed her mind.

"Oh! no," said I, "that will render Bosvil too happy: I will go home and write the whole scene of this treachery and make myself the last actor in the tragedy."[36] Perhaps the result of this perfectly natural proceeding was the first rough draft of *Bosvil and Galesia*, which may have been written up into its present form, later in life, when she had the tranquillity in which to recollect her emotion. At any rate it is a surprise to the reader to come across this simple tale of ordinary life at the end of her *Exilius*, with all its mediaeval paraphernalia of rudderless boats, hermits' caves, and marvels on every page. For there is no story at all but a girl kept on tenterhooks by an elusive lover who fails her in the end—a fit theme for the modern novelist, but in the early eighteenth century, amazing enough. And while *Exilius* leaves us colder than most of its kind, *Bosvil and Galesia* holds the attention. Jane Barker did not know her heroines of ancient Rome—that she calls them "young ladies" is, in itself, a proof of this; but she could write of herself with perfect frankness and without the restraint which a sense of humour might have imposed.

The passion of Galesia for Bosvil begins at the age of fifteen. "The first moment I saw this man I loved him," she writes,[37] "though he had nothing extraordinary in his person or parts to excite such an affection." Here is the first phenomenon—a hero with "nothing extraordinary" about him. He is in fact a very ordinary philanderer; which fact Galesia realizes and makes efforts to overcome her feeling for him by venting it in verse, with a hope to become the Orinda of her time. "I followed my study close," she says,[38] "betook myself to a plain kind of habit, quitted all point lace and ribbands and fine clothes, partly, I suppose, out of melancholy—not caring to adorn the person slighted by him I

[35a] Jane Barker, *Patchwork Screen.* London, 1723. p. 21.

[36] Jane Barker, *Entertaining Novels.* II. *Bosvil and Galesia.*

[37] *Ibid.*

[38] *Ibid.*

loved, and partly out of Pride, vainly imagining the world applauded me." But her passion is not so easily overcome, as the bitterness of her verses shows:

> Nought but my own false Latin now I see,
> False verse, or lover, falsest of the Three,[39]

and Bosvil has only to come back, with a casual hint of his admiration for her to make her grammar rules seem "impertenencies" and send her back to her point lace and ribbands with a high heart. When, after sending her hopes up and down in this fashion for some time, Bosvil calmly proposes a friend of his as her husband, anyone will sympathize with her in her desire to kill him—"inspired by an evil genius, I resolved his death"[40]—though one cannot help laughing at the way in which she chooses to versify her desires:

> Why was I born, or why a Female born?
> Or why not piecemeal from my Mother torn?
> Why did not I with teeth or rickets die
> Or other accidents of infancy?[41]

What other heroine of fiction ever thought of teeth or rickets in the bitterest moment of her life? When after all this Bosvil falls ill, she, very humanly, would rather he died than live not hers, "However," she adds,[42] "I did not pretend to capitulate with the Almighty but asked his life *in general terms*, without including or excluding his person, which by intervals, I hoped might yet one day be mine." Her hope was never fulfilled, for when Bosvil recovered, he basely married someone else—and Galesia was left to live out the rest of her days with reading, writing, and farming as her means of finding indifference. So fond did Jane Barker become of the heroine she had thus created in her own image, that she returned to her in her later collections, the *Patchwork Screen* and *The Lining of the Patchwork Screen*. The latter, indeed, is nothing more than a compilation of moral tales, each built round some proverbial saying, and with little enough of *Galesia* to bind them together. But in the *Patchwork Screen* it is the autobiographical scraps which form the brightest patches, thrust in as they are between romantic stories and kitchen recipes. When we find

[39] *Ibid.*
[40] *Ibid.*
[41] *Ibid.*
[42] *Ibid.*

Jane Barker, naïvely telling one of her Cantabrigensian admirers all about Bosvil, or sighing in vain for letters from that indifferent gentleman, "saying he is unkind . . . ., Oh no, his letter's lost"; we wish she had taken more pains over her writing. Had the author acquired a sense of form, in her long apprenticeship to her craft, we might have had a really good autobiographical novel. As it is, we have to be content to hunt for two grains of wheat among two bushels of chaff.

The value of all her work is in the earnestness with which the author portrays Galesia's states of mind. Bosvil is only sketched and hardly speaks throughout the book; the rest of the characters are mere names. But Jane Barker remembered her own feelings and wrote them down at the risk of making herself ridiculous. She is no calm self-student, like the Duchess of Newcastle, taking a long view of her life and character as a whole. She is interested only in this one emotional crisis, and the fierce jerky style in which she writes of it shows how deeply she was affected by it. Galesia is a heroine—as far removed from the Mirandas and Isabellas of Mrs Behn as from Evelina or Cecilia—who falls in love "before the gentleman's love is declared" but with perfect propriety. Only to herself she is unreserved; and in making a romance, after the event, out of her own reactions to a certain very common experience, she is antedating, at least in spirit, a very common type of novel of our own day.

Little more need be added to the story of the novel written by women before *Pamela*. There is no reason to drag forth Mrs Penelope Aubin from the oblivion in which she has been allowed to be buried. And there is little to say even of a voluminous writer like Mrs Eliza Haywood, in her period before 1740, which has not already been said of Mrs Manley. She writes better stories than Mrs Manley, but her materials are the same—secret history and the "Power of Love." *Love in Excess*, published in 1719, sets the pace for the rest.

> 'Tis Love Eliza's soft affection fires
> Eliza writes but Love alone inspires,[43]

says the unknown poet in the verses "wrote in the blank leaf of Mrs Haywood's NOVEL" and reprinted with the rest of the eulo-

[43] Eliza Haywood, *Secret Histories, Novels and Poems*. 1726. I. Fifth. Title-page.

gies in the Sixth Edition. Here are all the scenes and devices which have already become familiar to the reader of romantic fiction—bedchamber intriques and midnight assignations, back-stairs and rope-ladders, duels and disguises. Here too, we meet the agressive woman in Alovisa or Idalia. Mrs Maywood's treatment of love is after the manner of Mrs Manley, only more detailed and on the whole, less unpleasant. By writing of love she hopes to have an universal appeal.

"Love is a topick which I believe few are ignorant of: There requires no aids of learning, no general conversation, no application: a shady grove and purling stream are all things that's necessary to give us an idea of the tender passion,"[44] she writes in the dedication of the *Fatal Secret, or Constancy in Distress*—though she does not stop short, as a rule, at the purling stream and shady grove as an aid to the imagination of the reader. By writing of love, too, she ingeniously discovers in her work a means of conveying a moral—as she states in the dedication to *Lassalia, or the Self Abandon'd*.[45]

"My design in writing this little novel (as well as those I have formerly published) being only to remind the unthinking part of the world how dangerous it is to give way to passion, will, I hope, excuse the too great warmth which may perhaps appear in some particular pages; for without the expression being invigorated in some measure proportionate to the subject, 'twould be impossible for a reader to be sensible how far it touches him, or how probable it is that he is falling into those inadvertencies which the examples I relate would caution him to avoid . . . . Now, I take it, the aim of every person who pretends to write (tho' in the most insignificant and ludicrous way) ought to tend at least to a good moral use." This is the old plea of correcting vice by displacing it, which Sidney started in his remarks on comedy in the *Defense of Poesie* and which has been echoed at intervals ever since. One doubts its validity, at least, when it is used of Mrs Haywood's novels.

In her own age she was regarded as an authority on the human heart. She has Sylvanus Urban's commendation.

> Women the heart of women best can reach,
> While men from maxims you from practice teach.[46]

[44] *Ibid.*, III. Dedication.
[45] *Ibid.*, IV. Dedication.
[46] *Gentleman's Magazine.* 1744. May.

Occasionally we feel that she is, indeed, writing from "practice." She can never mention matrimony without a thought of the Rev. Valentine Haywood, and when she pleads the powerlessness of human beings in love, she is trying to excuse, perhaps, the "little inadvertencies" of her early life. In so far as there is any characterization at all in her novels, we find it in the portraits of women. They are represented, with feeling, as the wronged and suffering sex. They retire to convents, die of broken hearts, or live to see their lovers married to other people. The two heroines of the *British Recluse*, Belinda and Cleomira, strike an original note by retiring from the scenes of their love affairs into the country "happy in the real friendship of each other." But on the whole her novels are conventional enough. Open any one of them at random, and you will find the same stilted amorous dialogue, the same love letters written in their invariable style to the "too lovely" or "too much adored" or "the too-charming and perfidious" beloved. We see the hand of M^rs^ Haywood, the dramatist, when in the height of their emotion the characters break into a language that is almost blank verse.

By all my sleepless nights and restless days,
By all the countless, bleeding agonies,
By all the torments of my bleeding heart,
I swear that you shall hear me,[47]

cries D'Elmont, hero of *Love in Excess*—and there are many other such passages, which have only to be arranged in metrical form to suggest a minor Elizabethan tragedy.

There is nothing in stuff of this kind to give it enduring fame, and the many novels between *Love in Excess* in 1719 and *Evoaii* in 1736, are more interesting as a record of public taste than for their absolute merit. M^rs^ Haywood could, and did, write better than this when she had another lead to follow, but these early romances procured her the favour of the public and brought in her livelihood and that was what she wanted. "There is M^rs^ Haywood's novels,"[48] says the vulgar milliner in Charlotte Lennox's *Henrietta.* "Did you ever read them? Oh! they are the finest lovesick passionate stories: I assure you you'll like them vastly." But this was in 1758 and Henrietta, a child of the rising generation, wisely turns down M^rs^ Haywood for *Joseph Andrews.*

[47] Eliza Haywood, *Secret Histories* I.

[48] Charlotte Lennox, *Henrietta.* 1758. I, p. 36.

The day of these "lovesick passionate stories" was soon over, but we can still see in the works of the early women writers the psychological novel in potentiality. On the one hand, we have the records of real life in the diaries and autobiographies; on the other, tales of a fictitious world, and already the strands of the two were twisting. Out of the Duchess of Newcastle's power of self-analysis, Jane Barker's frankness in recording her own emotions, Aphra Behn's knowledge of life, there is material to make a good novel. But their various gifts have still to be combined and their knowledge to be made articulate. The interest in real life is still not made part of the stuff of fiction. Jane Barker comes nearest, perhaps, to writing a novel in the modern spirit. Her point of view is modern, in that she makes the reader feel what is happening, through the emotions of the principal character. She has almost dropped the conventions of fiction, also; only the fanciful names and the stilted dialogue remain. But though *Bosvil and Galesia* may be an excellent portrait of its author, it cannot be called a good novel. It is, indeed, hardly more than a sketch, for Jane Barker was not capable of making the best of her material. The attempt is there, however, and in the attempts of all these early women writers we can see an approach to the new kind of character study, that marks off the modern novel from the old romance. Not one of them created a character so good as Sir Roger de Coverley, not one of them achieved a realism such as Defoe's, but in the matter of using their own experience as a foundation for fiction, they were at least as early in the field as the men.

## CHAPTER II

## THE EVOLUTION OF THE HEROINE

### 1. The Man's Heroine

"Women the heart of women best can reach," sang one of the many admirers of Eliza Haywood, and, on the face of it, this seems sound enough psychology. One expects that as soon as women begin to take an active part in literature, a change in the conception of female character will follow. Up to the time when Aphra Behn began to write, woman's part had been a passive one. She had been content to inspire the poet, to play the model to the artist. The heroine of seventeenth century romance is essentially a man's creation, born of the masculine ideal of womanhood of different ages. Her pedigree is interesting and complicated. It dates back to the mediaeval world. Among her ancestors are those delicate ladies who wandered inviolate through the forests and gave a *raison d'être* to knight-errantry, as well as the regal patronesses of the Courts of Love. The stock received new life from the Platonism of the Renaissance, when the lady becomes identified with the Idea of the sonneteers, a divinity to be worshipped with a love that is immaculate. It was a form of this Platonic love, living on in the code of the *Précieuses* of seventeenth century France, that was the direct inspiration of Honoré d'Urfé's *Astrée*; and it was the *Astrée* that set the fashion for the ponderous romances that became so popular in England.

By this time the heroine of fiction was become a purely conventional figure. How remote from life she was, one has only to read the *Female Quixote* to realize. In this book the would-be heroine is introduced into the midst of a group of people leading ordinary lives, and thus her standards of romance are brought into contact with the standards of reality. Poor Arabella never has a chance among those prosaic mortals, her relatives. She writes a letter in the best romantic style to her lover with the direction, "The unfortunate Arabella to the most ungenerous Glanville,"[1] only to be reproved by an unsympathetic uncle who says, "I don't choose my messenger should know that you are unfortunate or that my nephew is ungenerous." She announces her heroic intention to emulate Mandana, who would not hear her servant's vows until he had spent ten years in silent suffering, only to provoke from her cousin the very pertinent comment: "Did she consider what alteration ten years would make in her face?"[2] Arabella can find no one who will play at the same game with her, and yet she could quote chapter and verse to justify her every action—from the Scudérys. There is not one of her vagaries which has not its precedent in the life of Statira or of Clelia.

Arabella's intense admiration for these ladies, intended as it was to ridicule the romantic notions of the girl reader of the period, makes us wonder how far they were real to the people who read of them. The reading of fiction affords us different degrees of pleasure. The deepest enjoyment, perhaps, is experienced when we can say, "This has happened to me." We feel enjoyment of

[1] Charlotte Lennox, *Female Quixote*. I, p. 59.

[2] *Ibid.*, p. 169.

another kind in the novel of which we say, "This *might* happen to me"; such is the appeal of half the cheaper magazine literature no less than of the tales of adventure which delighted us in our childhood. There is yet a third type of novel—that of which we say, "This has never happened to me, and is never likely to happen to me," but from which we still derive a certain pleasure. It must have been in this last class that the French romances belonged, for we cannot imagine that even the most credulous reader could have entered into the feelings of these heroes and heroines as real beings. They must have been accepted to begin with as something apart from life and tried by standards which seemed proper to the world of fiction.

What, then, did these accepted standards demand of the heroine? Beauty, of course, is the first essential—many years would have to pass before it entered into a writer's head to create a heroine without beauty. With her beauty there generally went an aloofness, an indifference to her lovers' sufferings— a quality which she inherited from her ancestors of the Courts of Love, who expected endless service without holding out a hope of reward. Heroines of romance were exempt, as a rule, from all the vulgar feelings of passion: their office was merely to accept the love of others. Their other qualities are high-sounding enough—they are "virtuous," "noble," "excellent," but the evidence of these qualities is chiefly in the author's word. There is an uncertainty, too, about the intellectual gifts of the heroine. She has always, vaguely, "Mind"—sometimes "all the excellencies of mind"; but one is tempted to think that these are catchwords and phrases. "Mind" had been a part of the necessary equipment of the Renaissance lady who inspired Platonic love. In Italy especially women had been honoured for their intellectual gifts, as bears witness the *Book of the Courtier* and the lives of the great ladies who inspired it. "Mind" was still a desirable quality in woman when d'Urfé wrote his *Astrée*, for though the women of his circle lend themselves easily to ridicule, there was much good sense behind the preciosity of the Hôtel Rambouillet. But by the end of the seventeenth century one imagines that the ascription of mental excellency to the heroine had become an automatic process. It does not mean either that the author or the reader demanded intellectual superiority in the heroine. Even M^rs^ Manley's nonentities have "mind." It appears in the opening paragraph of description, along with the beauty of face and symmetry of figure of the heroine and appears no more throughout the rest of the book. One cannot, in any way, take the heroines of this type of fiction as representing a living ideal any more than one can take them as a representation of life. They represent an old ideal and a foreign one. To find the true heroine of the period we have to pass on to the novels in which Englishmen are writing from their own thoughts and experiences.

A thing which strikes us at once is that for many years there are no heroines. From *Parthenissa* to *Pamela* there is a gap in their history. This period, as we have already seen, was one in which men paid little attention to women at all except, occasionally, to laugh at them. The only characters of women in the literature of the early eighteenth century apart from those to be found in the comedies and the slight sketches of the periodicals are in the novels of Defoe. Roxana and Moll Flanders are no heroines, but they are the most outstanding portraits of women up to the time of *Pamela*. Perhaps it was in reaction from the unreality of the conventional good woman of literature that Defoe sought after realism by making his chief characters a prostitute and a thief; but whatever the reason, Roxana and Moll remain a hundred times more real in their wickedness than Mandana and Astraea in their "unparalleled purity." There is nothing essentially feminine about them. Moll's story, in the latter part especially, where we feel the horror of her growing degradation, is an excellent study of the psychology of the thief, but there is nothing which would not have been equally applicable had the thief been a man. Roxana's life is the life of the prostitute of all ages. Except in moments, Roxana is hardly an individual. She gives us a naked, unadorned account of the workings of the instinct which we call *nostalgie de la boue*, but she does not invest herself at the same time with a distinct personality, as Des Grieux, watching the same instinct at work in Manon, makes us feel that she is indeed a person. Both Roxana and Moll Flanders exist only in the events that happen to them, and it is because of the unusual nature of these events that these characters escape from the ruck. Plot was still the first essential of the novel, as it had begun by being its very life; sentiments were the next addition, and character the last development. Moll Flanders and Roxana are characters only as the public figures in the newspaper are characters to us. Defoe has all the appearance of getting inside his people, of writing from within of their feelings and motives, but, in the end, the reader feels that the process of analysis is going on from outside. The fascination of *Moll Flanders* is only that of a longer, more unified coney-catching pamphlet. When we come to the women characters of Richardson's novels, we realize Defoe's limitations.

It is a well-known fact that Richardson, while still in his teens, occupied the position of confidant and letter writer to a group of young women. "He was fond of two things which boys have generally an aversion to," says M^rs^ Barbauld, "letter writing and the company of the other sex"; and these preferences of his boyhood determined the bias of his novels. The opportunities he had of studying the minds of the ignorant illiterate country girls in the Derbyshire village where he passed his early life stood him in good stead when he came to write *Pamela*. Not that Pamela is ignorant or illiterate. Richardson departs from convention to the extent of making her a poor girl and a serving-maid, but he endows her with "fine natural parts" and an "inoffensive wit." Her birth is a descent indeed from that of the princesses and noble ladies who have hitherto filled the pages of the novel: she is of genuinely humble parentage—not even a changeling, or a foster child stolen in infancy. She still has all a heroine's share of beauty, but Richardson is careful to point out that her beauty is the least of her attractions. It was her beauty that first brought her to the notice of M^r^ B---- but it was more than that which made him marry her. What this was, M^r^ B---- himself calls her "mind," and we come back again to this ambiguous word which seems inevitable in the description of a heroine.

If it were, indeed, "mind" in Pamela that won M^r^ B----, the word would seem to mean a certain low cunning coupled with a complete absence of pride. This is how Pamela strikes a modern reader. But we know very well that Richardson did not intend to convey this impression. To him Pamela's resistance to M^r^ B----'s project of making her a "vile kept mistress" and her change of face immediately the same man talked of marriage was entirely meritorious. It was in fact virtue rewarded—though the virtue might be in worldly wisdom and the reward in worldly goods. Pamela's conduct, to Richardson, was founded on Christian principles and it is moral principle that he implies whenever he talks of "mind." A high standard of conduct, and the steadiness never to deviate from this standard is what Richardson chiefly demands of his women. It is because Clarissa deviates from it, for a moment, that she brings her tragedy upon herself, as it is the excellencies of her mind which almost save her. It is Harriet's mind which marks her out for Sir Charles from all the other women who are dying for love of him: it is her mind which subdues even the more frivolous Greville, for it is he who writes of her, "Who can describe the *person* of Miss Harriet Byron and her person only; animated as every feature is by a *mind* that bespeaks all human excellence and dignifies her in every air, in every look, in every motion?"[3] Clementina also is remarkable for her qualities of mind; even the intolerable Emily Jervois has mind. One evidence of a fine "understanding" —for Richardson also uses this word of his heroines—consists in knowing one's place, whether in the servants' hall or the family, and keeping to it. Another evidence is the capacity to argue reasonably on all occasions, however much one's feelings may be involved—hence Harriet's quite unnatural magnanimity towards Clementina. This "mind" is, indeed, a complex possession. It is not to be confused with mere intellect or wit, though intellect and wit, too, are allowed within limits in Richardson's women. It represents in literature an ideal of Richardson's age, and, especially, of Richardson himself. It typifies the change in the attitude toward women from that of the early days of the century when "mind" and "understanding" were mere words in the heroine's catalogue of charms.

In *Pamela* we have the first portrayal in the novel of the heroine as a woman of wit. Wit with Richardson had two implications. It meant, on the one hand, a certain liveliness and readiness to reply, which he generally calls "pertness" or "sauciness." It is only in a measure that he gives this to his heroines. Pamela is her master's "dear saucebox." She can be pert enough on occasions, and even Harriet accuses herself of being saucy in her letters; but the chief exponents of this type of wit are Anna Howe, Charlotte Grandison, and Lady Davers. Though Richardson is indulgent to these ladies, calling their downright rudeness "charming spirits" and their merciless raillery "archness," the impression is that he feels they go too far. An "inoffensive vivacity," as Sir Charles calls it, is all he admits in the best type of woman. Humour he cannot give them, for he had none to give. But apart from this his women have the wit that manifests itself in self-confidence.

[3] Richardson, *Sir Charles Grandison*. I, p. 3. (*Works*. IX.)

Though in the stress of circumstances their physical weakness may overcome them, in a situation that can be settled in conversation and debate they show a capacity in bringing forward the right arguments which would do credit to a mature man. This no doubt is because they were using the arguments of a mature man. Richardson takes girls for his heroines and gives them the wisdom that comes of long experience of life. In all situations of life their judgment is invariably right—or what seemed right to Richardson. This is a trait which alienates our sympathy and makes us feel we have far more in common with Evelina and Camilla.

So far we have considered the general characteristics of Richardson's women—qualities which raise them above the generality of their sex and place them in the rank of heroines proper. We have yet to consider them as individuals. Pamela at least has a well-marked individuality. Richardson seems to have entered into her feelings and motives, her Servants' Hall morality, almost more than he knew, for the result is different from what we know he intended. He calls her artless and draws her scheming; he calls her innocent and shows her watchful and suspicious. As to the crucial point in the story, the yielding to M$^{r}$ B---- as soon as it becomes respectable, surely Richardson's own age cannot have been blind to the limitations of a virtue which dictated conduct such as that. One wonders how Pamela appealed to the women of the time. *Pamela*, the book, we know, was tremendously popular with women—they would like it, in any case, for its novelty, its sentiments, its discussions on the human heart—but what of "Pamela her own-self?" Men admired her, of course; it was inevitable that her attitude toward her lord and master should find favour with the majority of the male sex, but the encomiums of women are generally for Clarissa, for Harriet, even for Clementina, rather than for Pamela. Perhaps it was because they accepted her as a member of a class, of whose feelings they were ignorant, and concentrated their attention on the moral of the story that we hear little discussion of this very real character of the heroine. Pamela is a true woman—there are many little touches in her portrait that indicate a knowledge of women on the part of the artist—but she is a man's conception. If a women had been drawing Pamela, she would not have made her the heroine.

Clarissa is a different matter. Her story did not make all the women of her own and after ages weep, for nothing. She even drew tears from Lady Mary Wortley Montagu who disliked Richardson and disapproved of the book. Clarissa, unlike Pamela, has all the conventional qualifications for the position of heroine, for to beauty and "mind" she adds high birth and fortune. For a full list of her excellencies, we have Anna Howe's testimonial written after Clarissa's death, which may be simplified into the one fact that she had all the virtues. Such perfection does not prepossess us at the outset nor, throughout the shilly-shallying of the first book, does she win our sympathy. But from the moment when she surrenders herself to the protection of Lovelace, few could read her story unmoved. Her situation is lifted to a different plane and Clarissa herself magnified to the stature of a tragic actor. In the broken sentences of Lovelace's letter after he has carried out his crime, the tragedy reaches its climax. Clarissa has become something more than Clarissa Harlowe, daughter of James Harlowe Esq., country squire of Harlowe Place in Hertfordshire, as Tess is more than Tess Durbeyfield, the country girl, as Desdemona is more than the daughter of a nobleman of Venice. She transcends ordinary life and becomes a representation of human nature; they are more than the sufferings of an individual into which we enter. Clarissa is, indeed, more than an individual. When we look at her dispassionately, her faultlessness wears an air of unreality. She forfeits our sympathy because she remains cold of heart toward Lovelace. How much greater would her sacrifice have been had she loved him! She is overresigned in face of the unnatural treatment of her by her family. We are alienated by the persistent panegyrics of all who come in contact with her. Yet in the moment of her tragedy, all this is forgotten. One wearies of hearing her called always "angel" and "divine," but she remains something of what she was to her first ecstatic readers, "a thing enskied and sainted." One can only say that she is the conception of a great artist. I can think of no woman drawn by woman who is on the same plane with her.

Clarissa is Richardson's greatest creation and Pamela his most realistic portrait. Beside these two, the other women characters are unimportant. Harriet, even with the readers of her own age, had to share a divided allegiance with Clementina, and both are subordinated to Sir Charles, for whom they were created. Properly speaking, there is no heroine in *Sir Charles Grandison*, except as a courtesy title for the woman who is lucky enough to win the hero. Harriet's position is too undignified. She has to sit back until Sir Charles has made up his mind whether he will fulfil his engagement with Clementina and until Clementina has dramatically renounced her claim to him, and still to be transported by his belated proposals to the very height of felicity. Drawn from another point of view the situation could have been a good one, but the calm manner in which Richardson, and Harriet, take it for granted that she will be very lucky to get Sir Charles on any terms, and the manner in which all the Grandisons and Selbys and Shirleys stand round and sympathize with her place her in too humble a position for a heroine. Your heroine may occupy many positions but that of doormat must not be one of them. Harriet's excess of Christian charity towards Clementina, Clementina's magnanimity towards Harriet, Sir Charles's honourable love to both—all these strike us as unnatural. If rivalry in love is to be the theme of a story, at least one of the characters must be seriously in love and not in a position to reason and sentimentalize about his passion. Harriet is a far more interesting person before she falls in love. After she realizes that she loves Sir Charles, she becomes merely Richardson's ideal mate for his ideal man.

It was Richardson's boast that he knew the heart of woman perhaps better than woman herself knew it. "We must not always go to women for general knowledge of the sex,"[4] he wrote to Lady Bradshaigh. "Ask me now with disdain, my dear Lady Bradshaigh, if I pretend to know them. No I say, I only guess at them. And yet I think them not such mysteries as some suppose. A tolerable knowledge of men will lead to a tolerable knowledge of women." He had, indeed, a tolerable knowledge of women, though it was not through his knowledge of men that he approached them. He studied women direct. All his life he was in a position to carry on his researches, a position such as few men have occupied and few would have desired to occupy. Women dominate his novels. Where they do not, the result is less successful. He knew women better than he knew men—and yet, as he was a man, his women remain a man's creation. They have their touches of femininity—what Richardson himself calls "femality"—which we recognize as truth; but they are not the heroines to appeal to women as Elizabeth Bennett and Emma appeal to them. From the bare outlines of women sketched in the old romance, all remote from life and all

[4] Richardson, *Correspondence.* VI, p. 86.

alike, Richardson has given us full-length portraits complete in every detail, but they are portraits of women not quite akin to us. In the first place, they are still a man's ideal. As M$^{rs}$ Barbauld says in her biography of Richardson, "from his own beautiful ideas he copied that sublime of virtue which charms us in his Clarissa, that sublime of passion which interests us in his Clementina." Even Pamela is an ideal, though only an ideal serving-maid. And although women have their ideal heroines, too, and have no wish to see the characters of the novel mere copies of the people they see round them every day, they do not always take kindly to the man's ideal of womanhood. The preacher and moralist are too much in evidence in Clarissa and in Pamela. It is not merely that Richardson's women are faultless but that they are thoroughly conscious of their faultlessness. "How happy am I to be turned out of doors with that sweet companion, my innocence!" says Pamela: "My soul is above thee, man!" says Clarissa to Lovelace. We cannot complain that Richardson's ideal is a low one, but we feel he is making it a means of demonstrating to women their place in society. Richardson himself is always there, in the background. Men are capable, perhaps to a greater extent than women, of imagining and creating in literature characters greater than themselves and women should be grateful that he brought all "his own beautiful ideas" to their service. But, as in ideal conceptions we miss the pleasure of recognizing ourselves as we are, we demand at least the pleasure of seeing ourselves as we might be or would wish to be. In Clarissa, Pamela, Harriet, and Clementina we get what Richardson would have us be; and although women of his age worshipped the perfect, passionless heroines of his creation, we do not feel today that they represent a permanent ideal of womanhood.

After Richardson's elaborate studies, the portraits of women which we find in the other novels of the period seem only sketches. Richardson himself had nothing but contempt for Fielding's heroines. "Why," he asks, "did he draw his heroines so fond, so foolish and yet so insipid?" Beside the mature Clarissa, who before she was of age had learned to rule her life so that every hour of it was spent to some good purpose, Sophia and Amelia are, indeed, fond and foolish. Fielding himself, no doubt, considered them fond and foolish but he would not have allowed that they were insipid. Women such as Sophia and Amelia were those whom he admired. We have already seen that he had no use for the learned woman. M^rs^ Western to him was a woman who had been spoiled of her proper end, that for which women were created, which is marriage. There is no doubt that Fielding appreciated intellect in women up to a point—he was fond of his sister Sarah and probably enjoyed the conversation of his witty cousin, Lady Mary, but he could have dispensed with them rather than with the Sophias and Amelias who were his ideal. For the "not impossible she" who is to command his heart, Fielding asks beauty, constancy, and kindness. When he says of Sophia, "Her mind was every way equal to her person," he is probably enjoying a laugh at the expense of Richardson, for the whole description is in the mock-heroic vein. He is not concerned with Sophia's mind. She is beautiful and sweet-tempered, generous and courageous, fixed and faithful in her affections, and what more could man desire? Richardson calls her a "young creature" who goes "trapesing" about the country after her lover in what he considers a most indelicate fashion, but then, he adds, what can one expect of Fielding? "He knows not how to draw a delicate woman." But what seemed to Richardson a mark of indelicacy was to Fielding only an evidence of Sophia's worth. Her love for Tom Jones was the most important thing in her life, and the fact that she was ready to sacrifice dignity, family pride, and filial piety for love gave her the more value in Fielding's eyes.

Constancy, rather than chastity, is the virtue which Fielding chiefly admires in woman. "Women, to their glory be it spoken," he says in *Tom Jones*,[5] "are more generally capable of that violent and apparently disinterested passion of love, which seeks only the good of its object, than men." It is this love which makes Sophia take Tom, knowing his faults, and Amelia stick to Booth in spite of his lapses into infidelity. Where Richardson's heroines, clad in complete armour, would have rejected both Tom and Booth, Sophia and Amelia, no less pure in themselves, take them for what they are. Elizabeth Carter, though she was tolerant enough toward Fielding, could not quite appreciate the attitude of his heroines. "M^r^ Fielding's heroines are always silly loving, runaway girls,"[6] she says. "Amelia is an excellent wife but why did she marry Booth?" Why indeed do many women of Amelia's type

[5] Fielding, *Tom Jones*. II, p. 15. (Everyman.)

[6] Elizabeth Carter, *Letters to Catherine Talbot*. II, p. 69.

marry weak and shiftless men like Booth? That is a question that nobody can answer, but the fact remains that they marry them. Fielding accepted this as part of the natural order of things. He accepted the fact that Amelia should nurse Booth, housekeep for him, pawn her possessions for him, and love him in the end. It is not that he does not admire her for it; he does. But he knows that it was preference and not pure altruism that made Amelia stand by a man who was not worthy of her. Fielding believed as Johnson did, and as Richardson did not, that "women have fewer temptations, therefore greater perfection is required of them."[7] He belonged to the order of men who believed that women should be angels while men may be allowed to be sinners—a morality which persists to this day with many men—and he knew that the force of tradition is strong enough to make women as well as men accept this code. There is, therefore, nothing unnatural in the conduct of Sophia or of Amelia. They may be fond and foolish, as Richardson said they were, or the "silly loving" girls Miss Carter accused them of being, but girls of nineteen are apt to be foolish, especially when they are in love, and their silliness is truer to life than Clarissa's wisdom.

Perhaps they are a little insipid—it is not Sophia who is the central interest of *Tom Jones;* in *Amelia*, the greater prominence given to the heroine does not compensate us for the lack of Partridge, of Western, of Thwackum and Square; while *Joseph Andrews* gets along without a heroine at all, for the poor, artless Fanny can hardly be dignified by such a name. They have their moments when they capture our interest and sympathy. Every young girl will feel for Sophia over the incident of the muff, an indiscretion of which none of Richardson's heroines could ever have been guilty; and poor Amelia's sufferings are real enough in all conscience. But, although we do not dispute their naturalness, we cannot say that they are very interesting women. They are lacking in that which we call "character"—an attribute which we must admit is present in Richardson's heroines. The impression in the end, of Fielding's novels, as regards his treatment of the sexes, is that which we get from Milton's Adam and Eve.

> For contemplation he and valour formed,
> For softness she and sweet attractive grace,
> He for God only, she for God in him.

His heroines are, essentially, a man's conception.

[7] Boswell, *Life of Johnson.* (G. B. Hill.) III, p. 326.

Smollett's treatment of women is Fielding's, exaggerated and brutalized. His novels are, like Fielding's, men's books. The figures whom one remembers are men, Tom Bowling, Trunnion, Lismahago, and Matthew Bramble—those who play the character parts. As for the juvenile leads, they are duller than most of their kind. Richardson might better have applied to *Roderick Random* and *Peregrine Pickle* his criticism of *Tom Jones*, for the heroes of these are in truth the "lowest of all fellows" and the heroines worthy to be called foolish and insipid. The heroines, indeed, are among his woman characters in whom Smollett seems to have taken the least interest. Narcissa and Emilia seem to have been created only to be given in marriage to his intolerable heroes, Roderick and Peregrine, after they have got through the process of sowing their wild oats. Lydia, languishing over her romances and sentimentalizing over Nature in the absence of her lover, is a more sympathetic character, but even then, she could better be spared from *Humphrey Clinker* than almost any other of the chief correspondents. Fielding, in Amelia and Sophia, illustrated the truth that a woman will marry a rake and be happy, but when the rakes are as thoroughgoing young ruffians as Roderick, and especially as Peregrine, the women who marry them suffer a certain degradation. Far more pertinently might Miss Carter have asked, "Why did Narcissa marry Roderick?" for the weak good-natured Booth would seem to be cut out for a model husband compared with the man Narcissa marries. But the fact is we do not care whom Narcissa marries —or Emilia. They are beautiful young girls, gifted we are told, with "understanding" and virtue, but Smollett has not enough interest in them to make them interesting to others. He hands them over to rakes far less agreeable than Lovelace, without a qualm, on the assumption that, in providing them with a husband, he has given them all that a woman can desire. Fielding laughs at the unwilling spinster in Miss Allworthy and Mrs Western, but he laughs tolerantly. Smollett, when he talks of the "disease of celibacy" and the "competitors" who fought for Peregrine at Bath, carries his laughter beyond good nature. At the end of his life when he came to draw Miss Tabitha Bramble endeavouring to escape from her "most desperate state of celibacy," his cynicism has been toned down and the result is amusing enough. But in his earlier books his whole attitude toward women is so unsympathetic as to be revolting. He succeeds better with the women of low life—his women of the town, oyster wenches, landladies—Nancy Williams, Jenny Ramper, and M^rs^ Hornbeck. He is best of all, perhaps, in the characters of Miss Tabitha and Winifred Jenkins in his last book—pure comedy characters—who demand nothing more of us than that we should laugh at them. But Smollett is neither a feminist nor a student of feminine psychology. He is so far from seeing the woman's point of view in anything, that his novels are difficult, even, for a woman to appreciate. We do not look to him to help forward the development of the heroine.

Sterne has no heroines, as he has no hero except himself. The only woman who is drawn in any detail in *Tristram Shandy* is M^rs^ Shandy, and if she were to be taken as typical of Sterne's views on women, there would be no need to go any further. M^rs^ Shandy is a pale shadow of a woman, an echo of the great Walter Shandy, a wife in short, and Sterne had no use for wives. Jenny, who flits through the book like a spirit, but never appears, is nearer to representing Sterne's ideal. He was a lover of women but not of one woman in particular. "God bless them all," he says,[8] "there is not a man upon earth loves them so much as I do," and again he writes that he has been "in love with one princess or another all my life and I hope I shall go on so till I die, being firmly persuaded that if ever I do a mean action, it must be in some interval betwixt one passion and another."[9] One princess or another—it matters not who. Throughout the *Sentimental Journey* these princesses succeed one another and all, for the time, have Yorick's adoration. A lady met by chance at an inn, a beautiful *grisette* working at her ruffles in a Parisian shop, a fair *fille de chambre*—any of these can rouse the tender passion in him. It is the chance encounter in love which best fits in with his temperament. He wants no preliminaries, no consequences. All he asks of women is that they will accept his love for the moment and go on their way again. Love a woman and live with her all the days of your life, and she becomes in the end a poor pathetic ridiculous creature like M^rs^ Shandy. But love "one princess and another," and your love will be always young, your life full of romantic adventure.

[8] Sterne, *Sentimental Journey*. 1899. p. 187.

[9] *Ibid.*, p. 74.

Such was the attitude of Sterne. It was an attitude which armed against him all the moralists of the age, for it was not yet the fashion to grant full license to the possessor of what is known as the "artistic temperament"; it is an attitude rare at any time with the Englishman, who is more likely to follow the "wild oats" morality of Fielding, if he deviates at all from the conventional path. From the point of view of his treatment of female character Sterne influences the novel hardly at all. The women whom one meets in the *Sentimental Journey* are mere shapes who come and go and whose very faces we do not see clearly. While women were a strong influence in the life of Sterne, there are no heroines in his novels.

Having surveyed in brief the treatment of women in the four great novelists of the period, little remains to be said of the eighteenth century heroine as seen through the eyes of men. Goldsmith, in the *Vicar of Wakefield,* takes a conventional view, and makes the women inferior in every way to the men. Mrs Primrose is more notable for her skill in preserving and cookery than for her wit, and the "philosophical arguments" in which the men indulged are only counterbalanced by "innocent mirth" on the part of that good lady and her daughters. It is the women of the book who are weak in other ways also—wanting in judgment, easily led, easily deceived. But they are no more than slight sketches just as the whole book is only a sketch. Amory in *John Buncle* deals more at length with the characters of women. John Buncle, like Yorick, finds the society of women a necessity of life, only he demands more of them. He demands companionship and conversation, religious principles like his own, and a fortune enough to keep him. He is lucky enough in the course of his travels to marry seven ladies, answering to this description—one of them he marries twice—and to meet several others whom he might have married. These ladies are hardly differentiated at all, and they succeed each other so rapidly as to be bewildering; but they have one interesting point in common: they are all women of intellect and learning. It is no mere conventional "mind" that they possess. One of them, Charlotte Melmoth, can talk of "Cicero his Academics and De Finibus; or the English or the Roman History . . . . whether the Oedipus or the Electra of Sophocles were the best tragedy and the scenes in which Plautus and Terence most excelled."[10] Azora, head of that strange community of women at Burcot, leaves Buncle gasping by her fluency on all topics, from the herbs that made her salads to the flux and reflux of the Atlantic. "I never did hear anything like her!" says the poor man, quite confounded. We cannot pretend that his Antonias and Azoras are very convincing portraits of women—as indeed the whole book takes on a fantastic colouring that prevents our trying it by ordinary standards—but at least Amory's point of view is interesting. He demands of women intellectual companionship and the ability to converse like rational beings.[11] "Learning and knowledge," he says, "are perfections in us, not as we are men but as we are rational creatures, in which order of beings the female world is upon the same level with the male." It is unfortunate that he cannot bring home his argument to his readers by presenting his learned women in such a manner as to charm them and convince them. As it is, the reader might be justified in saying that if these are learned women, by all means let us have our women unlearned. Amory's views may have influenced the feminist; but we cannot pretend that they materially altered the conception of women in the novel.

No one, in fact, but Richardson really succeeded in creating a heroine who was a completely new type. Horace Walpole's high-born maidens have touches, but only touches of humanity, and we cannot see how he justified his claim that he was following either Shakespeare or Nature. Henry Brooke was far more concerned with his hero than with the woman whom he married. Fielding sketches his women in greater detail but he was only developing an older type—one that was already known to theatre-goers and readers of the drama. It is Fielding's idea of the heroine, we may note in passing, that persists in the great novels of the nineteenth century in Dickens and in Thackeray. But in Richardson and Fielding alike, different as is the angle from which they approach their women characters, we detect the masculine idea of woman. It remains to be seen how far the woman novelist departed from this idea.

## 2. THE WOMAN'S HEROINE

It is curious that, while the drama is full of individual figures, the characters of the novel should have remained so long at a dead

[10] Amory, *John Buncle.* 1904. p. 43.

[11] *Ibid.*, p. 347.

level of monotony, and that those who saw Rosalind and Millamant on the stage should have suffered as a matter of course the insipid heroines of fiction. It is curious also that, after novelists had realized the need for a closer approach to reality, they should not have been able to take their cue from the drama. But the fact remains that, for many years, the novelist was groping after realism without success. Women, as we have seen, were among the first to realize the need. Aphra Behn realized it, and tried to get away from convention by introducing her own experience. She succeeded in getting an effect of realism, also, by drawing wicked women, rather than good, and her villainesses stand out as their mediaeval ancestors stand out—those fierce, unscrupulous women who forged letters, poisoned messengers, and sent their victims out to sea in rudderless boats. Mrs Manley, also, was aware of what was wrong with the old romance. She knew, vaguely, that the women characters did not act as women act in life—as she herself would have acted. As she says, in the Preface to *Queen Zarah*, "It would in no wise be probable that a young woman, fondly beloved by a man of great merit, and for whom she had reciprocal tenderness, finding herself at all times alone with him in places which favoured their loves, could always resist his addresses; these are too nice occasions." Yet all that Mrs Manley could do to change this state of affairs was to pile up tremendous epithets in an attempt to convey to her readers the warmth of passion which consumed her characters. She exhausts herself over their feelings, but the fire from Heaven will not descend on them and they remain cold. None of the characters of these early novels can talk, and as long as we do not know them except at second hand, we are totally indifferent to their passions. Apart from the instances of autobiography already noted, there are no heroines in these early novels by women that attain to personality. Women were, perhaps, more restive than men under the old conventions, but they had to wait for a man's lead before they were entirely free.

Sarah Fielding was the first woman to write a novel after Richardson had set the new fashion in *Pamela* and *Clarissa*. *David Simple* is not a novel at all in the usual sense of the word. The sign which the author hangs out, after the manner of her brother, at the head of one of her chapters, might be taken as the motto of the whole—"Containing such a variety as makes it impossible to draw up a bill of fare, but all the guests are heartily welcome and I am in hopes every one will find something to please his palate."[12] The bill of fare is, indeed, various, for it contains allegory and satire, tragedy and comedy; love and honour for the romantic reader and wise observations for the moralist. The combination of so many themes—loosely connected as they are by the character of David Simple—results in a divided interest. We are dragged away from the love scenes of David and Camilla to hear the melodramatic, irrelevant story of the unfortunate Isabella; we turn from a moral tale like that of Corinna and Sacharissa to the picaresque narrative related by Daniel Simple on his deathbed. We are never allowed to get up a deep interest in any of the characters. Character-drawing, indeed, is not Miss Fielding's chief gift. She had a wide knowledge of life and a good deal to say about it, but out of her analysis of people and manners she could not produce a synthesis. *David Simple* is full of shrewd observations, but they are set down as in a notebook. Half her characters are pure types—mouthpieces for her own comments—and, when she comes to create a character who is not a type, the result strikes us rather as a compound of various characteristics than as a person. We know that she is consciously aiming, too, at drawing her characters from within. In her *Lives of Cleopatra and Octavia*, she is attempting, not to write an historical narrative, but to get at the workings of the minds of two famous women, gone "home to shades of underground." The result is not convincing. Cleopatra calmly talking of her wiles, as of skill in a game, Octavia complacently congratulating herself on her innocence make up a study in black and white with none of the half-tones of life. Even in *The Cry*, a most undramatic fable in spite of its title, the author states that her aim is "to paint the inward mind." Yet, in the end, all her characters have the drawback of the characters of romance in that they are incapable of conversation. They can talk to the extent of making speeches or relating histories, but they cannot converse. The conversation of novels is never quite the conversation of real life; but it is an artist's version of it. Miss Fielding's characters tell each other their thoughts, they argue and discuss, but they do not really talk unless the author herself has something to say, and even then they speak every one the same language.

The women, however, triumph over this impediment better

[12] Sarah Fielding, *David Simple*. 1904. Book IV, Chapter III.

than the men. Cynthia and Camilla are the truest to life of any characters in the book, and in Cynthia, especially, we have what probably represents Sarah Fielding's ideal woman. She does not trouble to describe Cynthia's person. "Perhaps it may be expected," she says, "that I should give some descriptions of the persons of my favourite characters, but, as the writers of novels and romances have already exhausted the beauties of Nature to adorn their heroes and heroines, I shall leave it to my readers' imagination to form them just as they like best."[13] It is Cynthia's mind—and truly enough in this case—that is her chief attraction. Cynthia, indeed, with her "advanced" views on women's education and women's position in society, her keen interest in what is going on around her, and her intellectual outlook on life, strikes us as having more sense than any other character in the book. She is, like Miss Fielding herself, a detached observer of life. It is into her thoughts rather than her emotions that we enter—thoughts, however, not as the stream of impressions into which we penetrate in the modern psychological novel are thoughts, but judgments and conclusions. Camilla is of a slightly different type in that she is endowed with greater sensibility. She has touches of human feeling which show that there was nothing hard or cold about Miss Fielding and that she had observed the ways of human beings in love. Camilla is human enough to be jealous of Cynthia, though she feels towards her a friendship which is rivalled only by that of Miss Howe for Clarissa. And it is a natural touch which makes her enter more and more into David's sentiments as her attachment to him increases. "Camilla had lately," says the author, "I do not pretend to say from what motive, been very apt to enter into David's way of conversation."[14]

But Sarah Fielding's heroines suffer from the fact that they are placed in a position between romance and reality. They still have about them too much of the atmosphere of an earlier world. Camilla's early life is as adventurous as that of a Mrs Haywood character, yet she marries the ordinary middle-class David, son of a prosaic London merchant. After the duels and suicide of the story of Isabelle Stainville, we come across a humble image from everyday life like the following: "And now, reader, if you are inclined to have an adequate idea of David's raptures,

[13] *Ibid.*, p. 346.
[14] *Ibid.*, p. 217.

think what pretty miss feels when her parents wisely prefer her, in their applause, to all her brothers and sisters: observe her yet a little older, when she is pinning on her first manteau and petticoat: then follow her to the ball and view her eyes sparkle and the convulsive tosses of her person, on the first compliment she receives . . . ."[15]—and this occurs at the culminating point of a love story. How Mrs Haywood or Mrs Manley would have scorned a comparison so lowly!—especially when the heroine was called Camilla and had fled romantically from her home. We are at a loss whether to regard Camilla and Cynthia as the conventional romantic types or as people like ourselves. In the end we do neither. Sarah Fielding had a better brain than her predecessors and a higher conception of women's understanding; for this reason her heroines are far above those earlier types, whose one experience of life was love in excess. But she cannot recreate her knowledge of the human heart, and her heroines are not women with whom one can identify oneself.

Mrs Haywood, with talents in many ways inferior to Sarah Fielding's, came nearer in the novels of her latter years to creating characters who were real people. She shows herself conscious of a departure from her old style in the Introduction to *Life's Progress through the Passions, or the Adventures of Natura*, published in 1748. No character, she says, should be portrayed as wholly virtuous or wholly vicious "for the human mind may, I think, be compared to chequer-work, where light and shade appear by turns . . . . I am an enemy to all romances, novels and whatever carries the air of them . . . . and, as it is a *real*, not fictitious character I am about to present, I think myself obliged . . . . to draw him such as he was." In what follows she defines, if unconsciously and ungrammatically, the appeal of the psychological novel. "Few there are, I am pretty certain," she says, "who will not find some resemblance to himself in one part or another of his (the hero's) character."

In the *Adventures of Natura*, however, Mrs Haywood does not quite live up to her promise. Natura is, indeed, compounded of human passions, but they are not sul ly mixed as in the living person. He is, in fact, a figure on a chart rather than a person—and the chart in this case is an illustration of the old Faculty psychology. Perhaps Mrs Haywood wrote after reading Locke or

[15] *Ibid.*, p. 337.

some popular interpretation of him—even Pamela on Locke—for her book reads like an early non-technical psychological treatise rather than a novel. Natura suffers one passion after another with a quite unnatural thoroughness and ends, as he should, with Reason on top and all his lower appetites subdued. But while the reader may "find some resemblance to himself in one part or another" as Mrs Haywood promises, it is only in one part or another. The whole man remains as unconvincing as his Name—a psychologist's Everyman, who is really No Man.

But when Mrs Haywood tried to draw a woman instead of a man, she succeeded better, and her investigations into the raw material of psychology now stood her in good stead. Betsy Thoughtless and Jenny Jessamy are both something more than lay figures. Betsy is not a sympathetic character for a heroine. If Richardson objected to Sophia and Amelia on the ground that they lacked delicacy, one wonders what he thought of Betsy—if he ever got as far as to read Mrs Haywood at all. Sir Walter Raleigh in his *English Novel* called her "own cousin to Roderick Random," and he was not unjust to her. She is, indeed, a vain, frivolous and thoroughly silly girl without any endearing traits to counterbalance her weaknesses. She has neither qualities of heart nor of head, but only beauty to make her attractive; and it is only in comparison with her really vicious and unscrupulous associates, Miss Forward or Flora, that she passes muster at all. But the point is that she is a complete departure from the earlier heroines of romance. She is the modern girl of her period, brought up in an English boarding school and turned loose in the London that Mrs Haywood knew. Her lovers are city merchants, men about town, Oxford undergraduates, and their love-making is carried on in up-to-date fashion. When one of them drops into the language of romance in paying his addresses, Miss Thoughtless interrupts him with a laugh. "I wonder how such silly ideas came into your head,"[16] she says, "shady bowers! and purling streams! Heavens! how insipid! Well," continued she, "you may be the Strephon of the woods, if you think fit; but I shall never envy the happiness of that Chloe that accompanies you in these fine recesses. What! to be cooped up like a tame dove, only to coo, and bill, and breed? O, it would be a delicious life indeed!"

[16] Eliza Haywood, *Betsy Thoughtless*. 1751. I, p. 106.

Here is a speech which is indeed in the modern manner—an illustration of Miss Rose Macaulay's thesis in *Told by an Idiot*, that every age has its New Women and that all these New Women are, in essentials, the same. Margaret of Newcastle had voiced Betsy's objection to marriage years ago, and, years after, it was to be voiced again in the *Doll's House*, and in books, indeed, without number. But the whole conception of Betsy is vitiated by the author's coarseness of grain. She makes her young heiress just such a romp as she herself had been in her youth, and gives her no charm to compensate for her lack of moral fibre. It is not surprising that M^rs Haywood should draw a girl of this type, when she got away from the conventional heroine. What is surprising is that she rose above it in *Jemmy and Jenny Jessamy*, which seems to me to be a much better book about much more agreeable people.

Jenny Jessamy is one of the first examples of the perfectly ordinary "nice" girl, as heroine of a novel. She is not, indeed, a heroine in the sense that she has anything heroic about her—as the ladies of romance were heroines, or as Clarissa was a heroine. She deserves the title only as she is "*our* heroine"—the character in the novel with whom we are most in sympathy, as Emma or Catherine Morland is a heroine. Jenny is a pleasant, amiable, sensible girl with a good heart and sound principles. Her love story, apart from a few inessential incidents, such as the duel, put in to delay the climax and spin out the novel into three volumes, is an episode out of everyday life, that might happen at any period. Jenny and Jemmy, like Betsy, are modern lovers, only their emotions are described with far more delicacy and feeling. Perhaps M^rs Haywood had been reading *Amelia* in the meantime, perhaps she owed something, too, to Charlotte Lennox; but, whatever the reason, there is a change in atmosphere from *Betsy Thoughtless*, in keeping with the growing refinement of the manners of the age. Jemmy, a weaker character than Jenny, has some episodes in his career which might distress the moralist, but he is far from being a profligate; he is hardly even a rake. There is nothing revolting about his infidelities, nothing to make us regret that Jenny should marry him. We should be disappointed, in fact, if Jenny and Jemmy did not marry, so natural and understandable is the whole situation. This is one thing that marks off the whole book from *Betsy Thoughtless* and from M^rs Haywood's earlier works. Marriage is no essential factor in the romances, it is all one to us whether the heroines are married or buried in the final chapter; and Betsy we have not enough interest in to care whether or not she marries or who marries her. But the conventional happy ending of *Jemmy and Jenny* is perfectly in place. It is a mark of the type of fiction which was popularized in the eighteenth century and which still survives, though it is out of fashion in our own times, a story of youth and love which leaves the hero and heroine on their wedding day. No one could call *Jemmy and Jenny Jessamy* a good novel. It is badly put together, it has many unnecessary and tiresome intrigues and half its characters are mere cyphers. But Jenny herself is interesting as an individual. She is a heroine of a new type, a person who is pretty and likable without being in any way dazzling or extraordinary, one whose feelings we can understand, because she does not have adventures remote from everyday life. Incidentally we may notice that though Jenny and Jemmy share the distinction of having the book named after them, it is Jenny who is the stronger and more interesting character.

When we come to the novels of Charlotte Lennox, we feel the presence of an intellect keener and more comprehensive than that of M^rs^ Haywood, and, at the same time we recognize that the author was more truly a novelist than Sarah Fielding. Charlotte Lennox is, indeed, a novelist who has not had her share of attention and one who, in these days of reprints, might well be reprinted. Her first novel, however, the *Life of Harriot Stuart Written by Herself,* would be no strong recommendation to a modern editor. Lady Mary Wortley Montagu was not far wrong when she said there was "a fool and jilt on every page," and fool and jilt in chief is the heroine herself. Harriot is only another Betsy Thoughtless translated to a higher social sphere. Her story lacks even the probability of Betsy's with its violent adventures and high-flown sentiments. When Harriot at the age of thirteen refuses a lover in the words, "I hate him with the utmost inveteracy. I can never look upon him but as a base incendiary," she sets the key for the whole piece, which plays itself out in similar style, up to the moment when the last despairing suitor strikes an attitude and exclaims, "I resign you from this moment to the deserving Dumont!" This sort of thing takes us back to the romances, yet, as the story is supposedly an autobiography and Charlotte Lennox cannot escape from putting something of herself into her heroine, Harriot has her moments of being a human being. One thing which strikes a new note is her fondness for children. On her visit to the Countess she leaves the general company because she prefers to play with the children in the nursery, an employment which would have been considered highly unsuitable for a romantic heroine. Another thing which we must notice in Harriot is that she is a well-read and educated girl. Like Sarah Fielding in Cynthia, M[rs] Lennox will not be satisfied with a heroine whose "excellencies of mind" are to be accepted only by hearsay.

*Harriot Stuart* may pretend to be a true history, but the heroine for all that is less natural and probable than the heroine of the farcical *Female Quixote*. Arabella is admittedly absurd, but, granted the initial improbability of her romantic code of manners, we find in her character a good deal of truth to nature. It must be admitted that a girl of Arabella's intelligence would not have persisted in living according to heroic standards, once she had seen that the rest of the world lived otherwise, but to make her realize her mistake too soon would have destroyed the comedy, which after all was the purpose of the book. And beneath her assumed character, Charlotte Lennox has contrived to show us the real character of Arabella. She suppresses her natural feelings because she is living up to an ideal, but they are there all the same. She loves Glanville from the first, only she has no precedent for accepting him as her lover; she will not allow him to speak of love and yet she is hurt when he does not show all that is required of a prospective husband. She is even angry that he should not appear jealous of her other admirers and there only needs a hint of his unfaithfulness, in the episode of the "distressed fair one," to make her suffer sincerely. Arabella has to occupy a difficult position in the novel. She is at once the sentimental heroine and the principal comedy character. On the one hand, she is a beautiful, generous girl with a good brain, only a little unbalanced, and a preference for intelligent conversation above the usual chatter of her sex. On the other hand, she is a ridiculous, undignified, and, in modern parlance, "impossible" young person who irritates and embarrasses her wretched lover beyond bounds. Yet Arabella's silliness, springing as it does from an overactive imagination, is infinitely preferable to the silliness of Harriot Stuart, which is a result, rather, of a flaw in character. Also, we have to admit that Arabella is very diverting whereas Harriot is merely tiresome.

Were it not exaggerated, as the plan of the book demands, Arabella's absurdity would be quite in keeping with the rest of her; it is the same thing, in a lesser degree, which we find in Catherine Morland and in her it is natural enough. Arabella is, in fact, the ancestor of a new type of heroine—one who can be intelligent and well read, and who still has her share of the foolishness incident to youth. Richardson's heroines, one feels, were never young, while Fielding's and the rest were never intelligent.

*Henrietta* is a less amusing book than the *Female Quixote*, but, as it is a straight-told narrative and not a satire, the heroine has a more serious claim on our interest. Henrietta is a better drawn example of the Jenny Jessamy type of heroine. She has more adventures than usually fall to the lot of young girls of her age, but otherwise she is not too remarkable to be believed in. Like Arabella she is a challenge to those who maintain the inferiority of women's minds and the foolishness of their conversation. When Miss Woodby, the coquet, declares to Henrietta that there is "inexpressible charm in the trifling chat of a pretty sensible fellow when we know he submits to it only to please us women,"[17] Henrietta replies, "Your sex is not obliged to you for that compliment. Must a man then talk nonsense to be acceptable to us?" Henrietta herself is not given to talking nonsense. She can dispute, on occasion, with a Roman Catholic clergyman on the subject of religion, and it is in consequence of this skill in argument and ready wit, that she has to leave the home of her aunt, who is trying to persuade her to marry a Catholic, and is turned loose upon the world as a martyr to her religion. Charlotte Lennox laughs at the spiritual vanity of her heroine on this occasion. She accepts Henrietta's priggishness as she accepts Arabella's romantic ideals, as part of their youthfulness. Here is the difference between her view and Richardson's. When his heroines utter high-sounding sentiments, he is taking them perfectly seriously, but, when Henrietta refuses in the heroic manner to comply with her aunt's wishes, Charlotte Lennox adds, "She was not free from a little enthusiasm that told her it was glorious to suffer in the cause of religion."[18] Henrietta's "romantick" refusal to change her religion, her desire to go out and earn her living rather than submit, her refusal of Lord B . . . . . . are all explainable on other grounds

[17] Charlotte Lennox, *Henrietta.* I, p. 111.
[18] *Ibid.*, II., p. 22.

than excess of virtue or religious zeal. When Henrietta falls in love, also, she behaves in a perfectly natural manner—as when Melvil goes away, "Henrietta who for a full hour had appeared animated with an extraordinary vivacity, became, all of a sudden, pensive and silent. *This change exactly commenced at the time Mʳ Melvil went away*."[19] Touches like this are in the manner of Jane Austen.

Mʳˢ Lennox's last heroine, Euphemia, is separated from the rest by more than twenty years, during which the author herself had had a hard struggle to support herself. It is not to be wondered at that she had lost her sprightliness when she came to write her last novel. Euphemia is a tired, faded heroine, married before the story begins to the vain, ill-tempered Neville, no substitute for the handsome young lover who is the customary fate of heroines. It is not in love affairs, indeed, that Euphemia's emotions are centred. All her feeling is for her children or for young people like Clara Bellenden. Her history is rather a book of memoirs than a novel, as the principal part consists in Charlotte Lennox's own reminiscences of her life in America. Looked at from this point of view, it is a not uninteresting document, with its sketches of Old New York, glimpses of Dutch houses and Indian settlements, its "froolicks" and sleigh-riding. But Euphemia herself is remarkable for nothing but her extreme ordinariness. We feel we have travelled a long way from the romance, when we have a married woman whose chief interest is in the nursery, for our heroine. It is interesting too as another instance of the fact that women made use of their own experience as material for the novel. When Charlotte Lennox was a young woman, recently married, she wrote of love and lovers' vicissitudes. In her later life she writes of the trials of marriage and the maternal sentiment and begins her maturer heroine's life where that of the younger ones ends.

We may say, then, that women were already in the process of evolving a new type of character before Fanny Burney began to write. They had broken with established convention (the *Female Quixote* shows how conscious they were of the break) and begun to embody their own ideas in the women they created. To some extent they were still imitative. They owed a good deal to Richardson, whom they followed in making their heroines women of education and of opinions of their own. But for this they only needed

[19] *Ibid.*, II., p. 192.

a precedent. Sarah Fielding and Charlotte Lennox, we have already seen, had strong views on the claims of their sex, and it was natural they should express them in their characters. They still owe something to the earlier fiction. As character developed, plot occupied a less and less important place in the novel, but Jenny Jessamy and Henrietta are not strong enough to make the incidents of the story subordinate to them and the authors still have to call in surprising adventures to their aid. But on the whole we see in the woman's novel the beginnings of a new type of heroine at once ideal and unheroic. She is raised above the ordinary but remains natural and probable. It is this type that Fanny Burney developed in *Evelina*.

We have already said that Fanny Burney began to write novels before she read them. It is probable that even before she wrote *Evelina*, she had not read much fiction of any kind. Whether she had read Charlotte Lennox we do not know. We do know that she had read both Richardson and Fielding and we recognize her debt to them; but what she took she changed and her departures from them are as striking as her borrowings. The story of *Evelina*, baldly stated, is pure melodrama. There is a long-lost brother, an implacable father, one of those nurses who, like little Buttercup, seems to have made it a common practice to substitute one child for another in infancy, in the end a dramatic reconciliation scene, and, to use a word beloved of M^rs^ Haywood, a general *éclaircissement*. Evelina herself, to judge from the opening descriptions, promises to be a heroine not very different from the Sophia-Narcissa type. She is endowed with great personal beauty, "gentleness of manners," an "excellent understanding and great quickness of parts." Yet out of such material Fanny Burney makes a natural-seeming story. How she effects it is in part explained by an entry in her diary—"I have not pretended to show the world what it actually *is*, but what it *appears* to a young girl of seventeen: and, so far as that, surely any girl who is past seventeen may safely do?"[20]

Any girl who remembered as well as Fanny Burney what it felt like to be seventeen, indeed, might safely overcome the worst difficulties presented by a rather unmanageable story. The vital moments in Evelina's life are not those when she rushes in to pre-

[20] Frances Burney, *Diary of Madame d'Arblay*. I, p. 2.

vent Macartney's suicide or meets at last the father who has never owned her—but the harrowing experience of her first ball or the agony of attending the opera in company with her undesirable relations. It was only from the maturity of five and twenty at most that Miss Burney observed her heroine; but twenty-five is far enough removed from seventeen to laugh at its crudity, and not too far past to acknowledge that it is the golden age. A person of twenty-five will sympathize with Evelina's terror at dancing with a man of fashion when she has never danced before but with a schoolgirl, at her running back to her seat when she heard the dance was difficult, at her paralyzed feeling of self-consciousness, when she feels Lord Orville is "resolved to try whether she was or was not capable of talking on *any* subject" and immediately becomes tongue-tied. Poor Evelina's first appearance in public, like Catherine Morland's, was not the success that a heroine's should be. She has the unhappy fate, in fact, of getting herself into ridiculous situations, neither romantically high nor romantically low, *unheroic* situations in which any girl may find herself. To an older woman the incident of Lord Orville's coach and the Branghtons might have seemed trifling, but to a girl of seventeen it meant intense mortification; to a maturer character it would have been all one whether Sir Clement Willoughby found out she was staying at a hosier's shop in High Holborn or not, but it is a serious matter to Evelina. Those who call her snob, forget that seventeen is an age for snobbery. She managed her relations with Madame Duval and the Branghtons about as badly as possible; but it was a situation to disconcert a much more experienced person. Clarissa, we feel, would have managed the affair perfectly, but Fanny Burney only gave to Evelina as much of knowledge of the world as was consistent with her years. She never forgets that it is from Evelina's point of view that she is telling the story. It is because he is seen from her point of view that Lord Orville is tolerable. Judged from his behaviour alone, he is both stiff and patronizing, but, as in Evelina's eyes he is perfectly desirable, we are bound to take an interest in her feelings towards him. There is something rather charming in the transparency of her early letters about him: "I did not wish much to dance at all—yet, as I was more acquainted with him than with any other person in the room, I could not help thinking it would be infinitely more desirable to dance again with him than with an entire stranger";[21] and again later in the book, when she thinks him unworthy of her love, and tries to persuade herself that her affection for him is only sisterly.

A naïve, romantic, unreserved young creature is Evelina, taking herself and the world with the seriousness of seventeen. She did not find the Branghtons and Mr Smith diverting—how could she? Were they not always there at the wrong moment to complicate her relations with Lord Orville and render her behaviour ever more unaccountable in his eyes? We may agree with Dr Johnson that the low comedy characters are the best part of the book, but not to see them through the heroine's eyes is to fail to appreciate Miss Burney's knowledge of psychology. *She* found the Branghtons amusing of course, but she knew that in Evelina's place she would have looked on them with different eyes. The early diary is a proof that Fanny Burney had found more material for romance than for amusement in the world when she was Evelina's age. In her excessive raptures over Millico, over Mr Garrick's acting, her sentimental interest in Hetty's love affair or Maria Allen's clandestine marriage, her desire to fall in love herself—in all this we see the foundation for a character such as Evelina's. *Evelina* is not autobiography, by any means, nor is Evelina herself merely Fanny placed in other circumstances; she is less witty, less precocious than Miss Burney in her teens. But Evelina has enough in common with her author to make the latter enter into her feelings. In part, perhaps, she is an idealized Fanny—what she might have been had she made her entrance into the world as a strikingly beautiful young orphan. We shall, indeed, often find that a woman's heroine is an idealized version of herself. But it is the fact that she starts from herself that makes her creation different from a man's ideal. A man might have been afraid to make his heroine a failure at her first ball or to make her ashamed of her relations.

Evelina is the most famous of Miss Burney's three heroines—perhaps because *Evelina* is a better book than either *Cecilia* or *Camilla*. These two have suffered because their histories run to a greater number of volumes with more sentiment and less humour. But the heroines themselves are not unworthy successors of Eve-

[21] Frances Burney, *Evelina*. 1893. I, p. 38.

lina. Camilla, indeed, is own cousin to her, though Madame d'Arblay was long past seventeen when she drew this later Picture of Youth. Camilla, young, artless and country-bred like Evelina with a genius like hers for getting herself into awkward situations, is obviously the work of the same hand. But she is no mere copy of Evelina. She has neither the extraordinary beauty nor the romantic history of Evelina to qualify her for the position of heroine. Men do not exclaim when they see her, "Good God! who is that lovely creature?"—she has, in fact, to occupy the position of foil to her more beautiful cousin Indiana—nor does she turn out, in the end, to be the lost heiress of an estate or anything more than the daughter of a poor country clergyman. She is, besides, of a different temperament from Evelina, more high-spirited, more impulsive, and in my opinion more charming. But the book stands or falls by the character of the heroine. There is nothing as good as the Branghtons, M^r^ Smith, or Madame Duval, for one cannot pretend that D^r^ Ockborne or even the egregious Dubster make up for these. All the interest lies in the vicissitudes of Camilla's love affair and for those who do not enjoy being kept on tenterhooks all for nothing, even that interest is soon over. For we are kept continually on the verge of an *éclaircissement* to be thrown back into suspense by an interruption in a conversation, a door opening, the entrance of an unwanted third party—and all because of a hundred little misunderstandings, which might have been avoided in an age of plainer speaking.

For those, however, who can see these trivial-seeming events through Camilla's eyes, they are not trivial at all. That her loyalty to her insufferable brother Lionel and her own inexperience bebetween them should land her again and again in predicaments in which she appears in the worst light to her rather priggish lover, Edgar Mandelbert, is no small matter to Camilla. She would be no true Picture of Youth if it were otherwise. Fanny Burney, here more consciously than in *Evelina*, is trying to analyze the states of mind of a young girl. She deliberately contrasts Camilla as she is with Camilla as she appears to others, and, while D^r^ Marchmont and Edgar are puzzled by what they consider a mixture of levity and steadiness of principle, fickleness and warm-heartedness in her conduct, we see her, as the author saw her, a perfectly natural girl. She is not drawn faultless; she is weak on occasions, extravagant, vain enough to want to be in the fashion—but there is no real flaw to hold her lover back. No one could condemn her, for instance, over the incident of the ball dress, when she persuaded herself that she was justified in buying a gown for which she could not pay because this great occasion was going to end all misunderstanding between herself and Edgar.

"When our wishes can only be gratified with difficulty, we conclude in the ardour of combating their obstacle, that to lose them, is to lose everything, to obtain them is to ensure all good. At this ball, and this supper, Camilla painted Edgar as completely restored. to her; she was certain he would dance with her; she was sure he would sit by no-one else during the repast; the many days since they had met would endear to him every moment they could now spend together, and her active imagination soon worked up scenes so important from this evening, that she next persuaded her belief that all chance of reconciliation being wholly upon the meeting it offered."[22] And so Camilla ran herself into debt for a dress of white lawn with lilac plumes to find in the end that Edgar did not come to the ball at all. Had he been present, indeed, we know that the white lawn and lilac plumes would have had little effect on him. Jane Austen knew this when she wrote in *Northanger Abbey* that "man only can be aware of the insensibility of man towards a new gown. It would be mortifying to the feelings of many ladies, could they be made to understand how little the heart of man is affected by what s costly or new in their attire; how little it is biassed by the texture of their muslin or how unsusceptible of peculiar tenderness towards the spotted, the sprigged, the mull or the jackonet."[23] But this is one of the things that women cannot be made to understand, and Camilla was only one with the rest of her sex. Fanny Burney is indulgent towards her foibles because she knows they are only the result of an impulsive generous nature, of inexperience confronted with the worldly gaiety of the life of an eighteenth century Spa. There is nothing wrong with Camilla though it takes Edgar Mandelbert some time to realize it. She is, in fact, a girl who might have come out of any country vicarage of her time, and one is sorry that Madame d'Arblay found it necessary to give to an ordinary tale a melodramatic ending.

Cecilia, who, in point of time, comes between Evelina and Camilla, is a heroine of another type. She is older and more mature

[22] Frances Burney, *Camilla*. 1796. III, p. 85.
[23] Jane Austen, *Northanger Abbey*. 1909. p. 57.

than either of them, a young heiress who is more capable of looking after herself than any of her appointed guardians are of looking after her. As she first appears to us, she is self-possessed and self-contained, a little like Elinor Dashwood in the "sense" she displays. But in the sensibility she develops after she falls in love with Mortimer Delvile, she is nearer to Elinor's sister. On the whole, Cecilia in love is a more human and attractive figure than she is at the beginning of the book. There are a good many natural touches in the portrayal of her character: her girlish heroics, for instance, when she makes up her mind to refuse Mortimer Delvile whom she thinks Mr Delvile, his father, is proposing as her husband, out of mercenary motives, and her sense of anticlimax when she discovers it is not his son but another man he is proposing. "Her heroic design of refusing young Delvile,"[24] adds Miss Burney, "by no means reconciled her to the discovery she now made that he had not meant to address her!" But, on the whole, Cecilia is a less attractive figure than either Evelina or Camilla. Perhaps it is because her adventures verge continually on the unreal and melodramatic. The episode of the Harrels, natural enough in the beginning, violates all probability in the Vauxhall scene of Harrel's suicide. Belfield's story is another incident which seems exaggerated and out of place. And, finally, the scene of Cecilia's renunciation of Delvile, when Mortimer exclaims, "Heaven then bless and hovering angels watch you," and Mrs Delvile adds, "O! Virtue, how bright is thy triumph," together with the whole episode of Cecilia's Ophelia ravings, suggest that Miss Burney had here read Richardson to no good end.

As for the heroine of *The Wanderer*, the exquisite Incognita, L. S., Ellis or whatever you choose to call her, she is hardly worthy to be mentioned beside these three. But one must say a word in passing on another of the women in this little-read novel, and that is Elinor Jodell, the ardent child of the Revolution who waves aloft the banner of Woman's Rights. So unconventional is she, so anxious to display her freedom from cowardly conformity that she casts off all modesty and proposes marriage to the man she loves.

"Harleigh, dearest Harleigh," she cries, flinging herself at the feet of the embarrassed Albert. "You are master of my soul. . . . .

[24] Frances Burney, *Cecilia*. 1782. II, p. 123.

Accept then the warm homage of a glowing heart that beats but for you; and, that beating in vain, will beat no more."[24a]

There is no need to say any more. If Elinor is interesting, as Fanny Burney's, or rather the middle-aged M^me^ d'Arblay's comment on Mary Wollstonecraft and her theories, she is also a proof that her old sense of humour had gone out of her.

One characteristic in common have all Miss Burney's heroines which cuts them off from us and places them in their century. I refer to their sensibility. What seems to us a weakness in the women of the time was to the age a virtue. It was by sensibility that your woman of refinement was distinguished from the herd as only the true Princess could feel the pea beneath the forty feather beds of the fairy story. We find it difficult to understand nowadays, why Evelina should go through such agitations and faintings before she met her unknown father, or scream and sink to the floor when she did meet him; or why Cecilia's brain should be almost unhinged even by the serious difficulties that surrounded her. The heroine of "exquisite sensibility," so boisterously parodied in *Love and Friendship* and so subtly in *Sense and Sensibility*, belongs to a bygone age. She represents an eighteenth century ideal of men and women alike; it is not until Jane Austen that we escape from the period of hartshorn and water. Mrs Radcliffe's heroines suffer from their sensibility. Charlotte Smith's are affected by it. "O dear sensibility!" cries Sterne in his *Sentimental Journey*, and he is invoking an eighteenth century goddess.

Such are the heroines of Fanny Burney. We cannot pretend, of course, to exhaust the catalogue of her gifts in speaking only of the young creatures after whom she named her books. She had the power of creating types outside herself, which is perhaps a rarer gift than that of creating character with self as a starting point. To do her justice, we should study the crowd of characters, old and young, high and low that fill her canvases—comedy figures like Smith and Dubster; Mr Meadows and Miss Larolles; mature women like Mrs Delvile and Mrs Arlbury; Mrs Mitten, Madam Duval, Mrs Belfield in all their different degrees of vulgarity. But she would have been an important writer for her heroines alone as they represent a different type from the man-made heroine. They are merely "nice" girls, moderately intelligent

[24a] Frances Burney, *The Wanderer*. I, p. 400.

—neither scholars like Eugenia nor fools like Indiana—affectionate and generous and ready to submit unquestioningly to the men who married them. They have not the wit of Emma or Elizabeth Bennett, for, although Fanny Burney had humour herself, she did not give it to her heroines. Nor are they modern women as Emma or Elizabeth is modern, for their self-reliance and independence. One feels they were created only to love and be beloved, and the inevitable end of their stories is always that of the *Princess;* "Lay thy sweet hands in mine and trust to me." Yet they are creatures for whom we have a fellow feeling. We see everything that happens from their point of view, and, because the author knew what she was talking about, we recognize the point of view as a true one.

After Fanny Burney there is little to be said of the heroine till we come to Jane Austen. M^rs^ Radcliffe's heroines are an old romantic type only with the fashionable quality of sensibility added to make them at home in their period. We do not recognize ourselves or our own emotions in the pensive all-accomplished Emily, in Adeline or Julia or Ellena. They are all the same with their taste for drawing, writing poetry, and, vaguely, "books." If they were changed about and Adeline instead of Emily were imprisoned in the Castle of Udolpho, it would make no difference to the story. They are all young, all beautiful, all excessively refined, all "tremblingly alive." It would be interesting, by the way, to count the number of times this phrase of Pope's occurs in the novels of the latter eighteenth century. It seems to have been as much taken for granted that the heroine of this period should be "tremblingly alive" as it was that her sister of a century ago should be beautiful. Charlotte Smith's heroines share this quality with the rest. They have a good deal, in fact, in common with M^rs^ Radcliffe's, as they owe a good deal also to Miss Burney. But there is nothing new in Emmeline or Ethelinde. They are a combination of all the qualities which heroines usually possessed—but they are not real people. They have their natural touches but, like M^rs^ Radcliffe's, in their total effect they are creatures from another world.

Enough has been said to show that there was a definitely feminine idea of woman before Jane Austen gave us a group of heroines which has never been equalled by any other novelist. In Miss Burney it was well established. Hazlitt, passing on to discuss her after discussing the great men novelists of the period, comments on her femininity. "Madame d'Arblay," he says, "is a mere common observer of manners *and also a very woman.* It is this last circumstance, which forms the peculiarity of her writings and distinguishes them from those masterpieces which I have just mentioned. She is a quick lively and accurate observer of persons and things; but she always looks at them with a consciousness of her sex, and in that point of view in which it is the particular business and interest of women to observe them. . . . . The difficulties in which she involves her heroines are too much 'Female Difficulties'; they are difficulties created out of nothing."[25] Hazlitt here seems to be quarelling with Miss Burney for her woman's point of view. Why he should object to this perfectly natural way of looking at things one cannot say. But the point is that he recognizes it as a fact—as Henry Fielding, years before, had recognized that no man could have written his sister Sarah's novels. "A very woman," "woman's point of view," "female difficulties," these are the things that mark out Miss Burney's novels, in his opinion, from those of the great men, her predecessors. Whether she wrote better or worse than they, she wrote a different type of novel and created a different type of character.

The question remains—is there any justification, from such evidence, for a belief in a different psychology underlying the work of women? On the whole, I think there is. The fact that a woman's observation of character starts from herself, and that she uses her feelings as a touchstone to test the feelings of others—an inevitable trend in woman's work from the first—is her chief strength as a novelist. Leigh Hunt notes this when he speaks of the "usual tendency of female writers to break through conventional commonplaces with touches of Nature,"[26] and says that "the least of them have an instinct of this sort which . . . sets them above the same class of writers of the other sex." It argues a great power of self-knowledge in the writer and a firmer hold on reality. On the other hand, it argues an inferior power of escaping from self and a weaker sense of ideality. Because woman sees herself and her own faults clearly she is less apt to be carried away by an ideal. This saves her, on the one hand, from imagining perfection where it is not, from magnifying a personal motive into something greater,

[25] Hazlitt, *Works*. 1903. VIII, p. 123–4.

[26] Leigh Hunt, *Men, Women and Books*. 1847. II, p. 131.

and rationalizing her own conduct where a reasonable explanation is out of place. On the other hand, it makes her unwilling to recognize or even incapable of recognizing motives greater than her own. It is rarely the women of the world who are the seers of visions and dreamers of dreams—either for good or ill. "What do you mean?" and "*Who* was it that thus cried," said Lady Macbeth when Macbeth, after Duncan's murder, was rapt by the sound of voices from another world. Women, it seems, are imaginative only up to a point. They are daydreamers, imagining themselves in all conceivable situations. But always it is themselves they see and almost always their daydreams keep within the bounds of probability. For such reasons the novel is their field—and the novel which sees the events through the eyes of one character in particular is, more especially, adapted to their genius. They can write of their own experience—the little things that men may not see, details that require the "microscopic eye," and while they are on their own ground, they are sure. Hence Jane Austen's "painting on ivory" which shows at once the perfection and limitation of the woman novelist's work.

It would be interesting to look back from a point in the future to see how far women's work has changed as their experience has widened. Then, indeed, we might be able to judge between the feminine mind and the feminine tradition. But whether or not it is through being kept in the dark, that women have acquired a different range of vision, whether education and experience will give them the impersonality and idealism which they seem to have in a degree more "mesurable" than men, the "very woman" in the past must have the credit of evolving a type of literature which has proved one of the greatest honours to her sex, and which has a unique place by virtue of its femininity.

## CONCLUSION

This study does not pretend to be complete or exhaustive. The inaccessibility of many of the works of these early writers has meant that some of them which might have been of interest have had to be excluded. Others, better known, perhaps, I have omitted because they do not seem to me to be of special importance from the point of view of this thesis. As regards their connection with the feminist movement, I offer only a few suggestions. That there is a connection, I think, is clear. When the Duchess of Newcastle wrote, the Duke spoke truth when he said of her works, "Here's the crime, a lady writes them," and we see the opinion of the educated woman of the period in Dorothy Osborne's comment on the same works: "Sure the poor woman must be a little distracted, she would never be so ridiculous as to venture at writing books." All this is changed by the end of the eighteenth century, and the change coincides with a general alteration in the status of women. They were emerging from the period of the "fair sex" and beginning to be considered as rational creatures. If we ascribe this change, vaguely, to public opinion, we must admit that it was the women themselves who helped to make public opinion. That the women writers were conscious of their position is shown in many ways: in the characters they create, the comments they make by the way, in the language, apologetic or challenging, of their prefaces to the reader. That the age was conscious of this change in position is shown equally by its praises and its hostility. It became too soon an automatic compliment to address the woman writer as the "glory of her sex," but even this conventional phrase had its foundation in the perception of the fact that the whole sex did, indeed, gain prestige from the few who won success in the field of literature.

With regard to the second aim of this study, the investigation of the works of women novelists with a view to discover how far there are certain "qualities of females" which give a special bias to what they write, this can only be a "conclusion in which nothing is concluded." Gossip about women is a fascinating pastime, but it is apt to end in airy speculation. The eighteenth century found it intensely interesting. The mere recurrence of the word "female" throughout the literature of the period is enough to show how much women came in for discussion. It was a word which had a special charm for them as it had also a special meaning. One comes across accounts in their periodicals of "Female Heroism," "Female Extravagance," "Female Inconstancy," as though heroism or extravagance or inconstancy were a different thing for being "female." They were more certain of their ground in those days than we are at the present time. They accepted a female mind and female genius as facts and, to the majority, their inferiority was a matter beyond question. They provided their women with *Ladies' Diaries*, *Ladies' Miscellanies*, and *Ladies' Libraries*, a special literature to fit their weaker comprehension. Their methods of education were based on the fact that women had one type of mind and men another. Nowadays the pendulum has swung in the opposite direction, and we are told that there is no difference, but only that the proof of this has to be deferred to a conveniently distant future. Perhaps Miss Rose Macaulay is right in her division of the world into Mental Males, Mental Females, and Mental Neutrals, and each generation, in the future, may produce a greater number of Mental Neutrals as the sexes participate more and more in the same experiences. Only, as we can never get away from the physical differences between the sexes and the differences, especially, between their nervous systems, it does not seem that there can be complete mental neutrality. Whatever happens in the future, however, the women's novels of the past would seem to belong to the Mental Females. It is hard to think that there may come an age incapable of appreciating their femininity.

It is hard, indeed, on those ladies who were once the ornaments of their sex, that they should now be revived only with the excuse of connecting them with a movement which is of interest to a Psychological and Sociological age. To those who, like the late Professor Raleigh, prefer a bad old book to a bad new book there is no need of any apology in unearthing these bygone authors. But the majority of people are so far from this view that they prefer a bad new book even to a good old one, and, to the majority, therefore, it must be confessed that these learned and ingenious ladies are as nothing. "The iniquity of oblivion blindly scattereth her poppy." Charlotte Lennox is buried in the same grave as the nine Miss Minifies and *David Simple* hardly escapes the fate of the

*Mausoleum of Julia.* And yet these women in their day were admired by no less men than Richardson and Johnson.

If this study has done anything to prove that the women novelists who flourished from the Restoration to the Regency are of interest either for what they wrote or for what they were, the time devoted to it has not been wasted.

# BIBLIOGRAPHY

## I

## Novels Read for This Study

### A. Novels Written by Women.

Aubin, Penelope
*Histories and Novels.* 3 volumes (title pages lacking).
*Illustrious French Lovers.* London, 1732.

Austen, Jane
*Works.* 6 volumes. London, 1909 (ed. Austin Dobson).
*Love and Friendship.* London, 1922 (ed. G. K. Chesterton).

Barker, Jane
*Entertaining Novels.* 2 volumes. London, 1736 (3d edition).
*A Patchwork Screen for the Ladies.* London, 1723.
*The Lining of the Patchwork Screen,* London, 1726.

Behn, Aphra
*Works.* 6 volumes, London, 1915 (ed. Summers).

Burney, Frances (Madame d'Arblay)
*Camilla.* 3 volumes. Dublin, 1796.
*Cecilia.* 6 volumes. London, 1782.
*Evelina.* 2 volumes. London, 1893.
*The Wanderer.* 5 volumes. London, 1814.

Fielding, Sarah
*Adventures of David Simple.* London, 1904 (ed. Baker).
*Familiar Letters between the Principal Characters in David Simple.* London, 1747.
*The Governess or The Little Female Academy.* London, 1749.
*The Lives of Cleopatra and Octavia.* London, 1928.
*The History of Ophelia.* Paris, "au Septième," (1799?).

Haywood, Eliza
*Betsy Thoughtless.* 4 volumes. London, 1751.
*Court of Carimania.* London, 1727 (2d edition).
*Jemmy and Jenny Jessamy.* 3 volumes. London, 1753.
*Life's Progress through the Passions.* London, 1753.
*Secret Histories. Novels and Poems.* 4 volumes (containing all works published up to 1726). London, 1726.

Inchbald, Elizabeth
*A Simple Story.* London, 1908.

Lennox, Charlotte
*Euphermia.* 4 volumes. London, 1790.
*Female Quixote.* 2 volumes. London, 1752.
*Harriot Stuart.* 2 volumes. London, 1751.
*Henrietta.* 2 volumes. London, 1758.

MANLEY, MARY DE LA RIVIERE
*Adventures of Rivella*. London, 1714.
*History of Queen Zarah*. London, 1711.
*New Atlantis*. 2 volumes. London, 1709.
*New Atlantis*. 4 volumes. London, 1720.
*Power of Love in Seven Novels*. London, 1720.

RADCLIFFE, ANN
*Castles of Athlin and Dunbayne*. Dublin, 1794.
*Gaston de Blondeville* (with selections from *Journals*). London, 1826.
*Mysteries of Udolpho*. London, (187?)
*Romance of the Forest*. London, 1897.
*Sicilian Romance*. London, 1809.
*The Italian*. London, 1797.

REEVE, CLARA
*Old English Baron*. London, 1820.

SCUDÉRY, MADELEINE DE
*Artamanes or the Grand Cyrus* (translated by F. G. Esq.). London, 1650.

SHERIDAN, FRANCES
*Nourjahad*. London, 1927.
*Memoirs of Miss Sidney Bidulph*. 5 volumes. London, 1786. (In *Novelist's Magazine*, Vol. 22.)

SMITH, CHARLOTTE
*Emmeline*. London, 1816.

B. NOVELS WRITTEN BY MEN.

AMORY, THOMAS
*John Buncle*. London, 1904 (ed. Baker).

BOYLE, ROGER (EARL OF ORRERY)
*Parthenissa*. 2 volumes. London, 1656.

BROOKE, HENRY
*Fool of Quality*. London, 1904 (ed. Baker).

DEFOE, DANIEL
*Works*. 16 volumes. New York, 1905.

FIELDING, HENRY
*Works*. 12 volumes. London, 1902 (ed. Saintsbury).
*Tom Jones*. 2 volumes. (Everyman)

GOLDSMITH, OLIVER
*Vicar of Wakefield*. 2 volumes. (*Works*, New York, 1900.)

RICHARDSON SAMUEL
*Works*. 12 volumes. London, 1883 (ed. Leslie Stephen).

SMOLLETT, TOBIAS
*Works*. 12 volumes. London, 1899 (ed. Henley).

STERNE, LAURENCE
*Works*. 2 volumes. London, 1885 (ed. J. P. Browne).

WALPOLE, HORACE
*Castle of Otranto*. New York, (no date).

## II

### LETTERS, MEMOIRS, AND DIARIES

D'ARBLAY, FRANCES
*Diary*. 4 volumes. London, 1891 (ed. C. Barrett).

AUSTEN, JANE
*Letters*. London, 1925 (ed. R. Brimley Johnson).

BOSWELL, JAMES
*Life of Johnson*. London, 1904 (ed. G. B. Hill).

BURNEY, CHARLES
*Memoirs of Dr. Burney*. London, 1832.

BURNEY, FRANCES
*Early Diary*. 2 volumes. London, 1907 (ed. A. R. Ellis).

CARTER, ELIZABETH
*Letters to Catherine Talbot*. 4 volumes. London, 1809.
*Letters to Elizabeth Montagu*. 3 volumes. London, 1817.

CAVENDISH, MARGARET, DUCHESS OF NEWCASTLE
*A True Relation of my Birth, Breeding and Life* with the *Life of William Cavendish, Duke of Newcastle*. London, 1886

CHAPONE, HESTER
*Letters on the Improvement of the Mind*. Boston, (no date) (ed. William Green).

CLIFFORD, LADY ANNE
*Diary*. London, 1923 (ed. V. Sackville-West).

DELANY, MARY
Selection from *Correspondence*. London, 1925 (ed. R. Brimley Johnson).

EVELYN, JOHN
*Diary and Correspondence*. no date (ed. William Bray).

FANSHAWE, LADY ANN
*Memoirs*. London, 1907.

HAMILTON, ANTHONY
*Memoirs of Count Grammont*. London, 1864.

HUTCHINSON, LUCY
*Autobiography* and *Life of Colonel Hutchinson*. London, 1863.

MONTAGU, ELIZABETH
*Letters*. 2 volumes. London, 1906 (ed. Climenson).

MONTAGU, LADY MARY WORTLEY
*Letters*. no date (Everyman).

MORE, HANNAH
*Memoirs*. 2 volumes. New York, 1837.

OSBORNE, DOROTHY
*Letters*. London, 1888 (ed. Parry).

PEPYS, SAMUEL
*Diary and Correspondence*. 4 volumes. Philadelphia, 1889.

POPE, ALEXANDER
*Correspondence*. (In *Works*. Elwin and Courthope.)

RICHARDSON, SAMUEL
*Correspondence*. 6 volumes. London, 1804 (ed. Barbauld).

SWIFT, JONATHAN
*Journal to Stella* and *Correspondence.* (In *Works.* 1883. ed. Scott.)
WALPOLE, HORACE
*Letters.* 16 volumes. London, 1903 (ed. Toynbee).

## III

## PERIODICALS CONSULTED

*Examiner* (in Swift, *Works*. ed. Scott. London, 1883).
*Female Spectator.* 4 volumes. London, 1771.
*Freeholder* (in Addison, *Works.* 1875).
*Gentleman's Magazine* 1732–97.
*Guardian* (in *British Essayists.* 1823. XIII–XV).
*Lover* London, 1906.
*Monthly Review* 1749–97.
*Rambler* (in *British Essayists.* 1823. XV–XVII).
*Spectator* (*Ibid.*, V–XII).
*Tatler* (*Ibid.*, I–IV.)

## GENERAL BIBLIOGRAPHY OF WORKS READ AND CONSULTED

ALGAROTTI
*Sir Isaac Newton's Philosophy Explained.* London. 1739 (translated from the Italian by Elizabeth Carter).
ASCHAM, ROGER
*Scholemaster.* New York, 1888.
ASHTON, JOHN
*Social Life in Queen Anne's Reign.* London, 1919.
BALLARD, GEORGE
*Memoirs of British Ladies.* London, 1773.
BURR, ANNA R.
*The Autobiography.* New York, 1909.
CIBBER, COLLEY
*An Apology for his Life.* (Everyman).
COWLEY, ABRAHAM
*Works.* 1684.
CROSS, WILBUR L.
*History of Henry Fielding.* 3 volumes. New York, 1918.
FONTENELLE, BERNARD LE BOVIER DE
*Entretiens sur la Pluralité des Mondes.* Paris, 1883.
GEORGE, W. L.
*Intelligence of Women.* Boston, 1916.
HAWKINS, SIR JOHN
*Life of Johnson.* London, 1787.
HAZLITT, WILLIAM
*Works.* 12 volumes. London, 1903.
HUCHON, R.
*Mrs Montagu and her Friends.* New York, 1907.

HUGHES, HELEN SARD
*Mary Mitchell Collyer.* (*Journal of English and Germanic Philology.* XV.)
HUNT, LEIGH
*Men, Women and Books.* 2 volumes. London, 1847.
JOHNSON, R. BRIMLEY
*Women Novelists.* London, 1918.
KAVANAGH, JULIA
*English Women of Letters.* 2 volumes. London, 1863.
KERR, S. PARNELL
*George Selwyn and the Wits.* New York, 1909.
MANWARING, ELIZABETH WHEELER
*Italian Landscape in England in the Eighteenth Century.* New York, 1925.
MARTIN, JOHN
*Feminism.* New York, 1916.
MONTAIGNE, MICHEL DE
*Essays.* 6 volumes. (Translated Florio.) London, 1898.
MOORE, F. FRANKFORT
*A Georgian Pageant.* London, 1908.
MORE, HANNAH
*Works.* 2 volumes. New York, 1837.
MORGAN, CHARLOTTE E.
*Rise of the Novel of Manners.* New York, 1900.
PERRY, H. TEN EYCK
*First Duchess of Newcastle.* Boston, 1918.
PHILLIPS, KATHARINE
*Works.* 1768.
PHILLIPS, MARGARET (AND W. S. TOMKINSON)
*English Women in Life and Letters.* Oxford, 1925.
PRIOR, MATTHEW
*Works.* Cambridge 1905.
POPE, ALEXANDER
*Works.* 10 volumes. London, 1871. (Elwin and Courthope.)
RALEIGH, SIR WALTER ALEXANDER
*The English Novel.* New York, 1896.
REYNOLDS, MYRA
*Learned Lady in England.* Boston, 1920.
SACKVILLE-WEST, HON. VICTORIA MARY
*Aphra Behn, the Incomparable Astraea.* New York, 1928.
SAINTSBURY, GEORGE
*The English Novel.* London, 1913.
SCOTT, SIR WALTER
*Lives of Eminent Novelists.* London, no date.
SQUIRE, J. C.
*A Book of Women's Verse.* Oxford, 1921.
STEELE, SIR RICHARD
*Ladies' Library.* London, 1732.
STEPHEN, LESLIE
*English Literature and Society in the Eighteenth Century* New York, 1907.

THOMSON, CLARA LINKLATER
*Samuel Richardson*. London, 1907.
WHICHER, GEORGE F.
*Mrs. Eliza Haywood*. New York, 1915.
WOLLSTONECRAFT, MARY
*Vindication of the Rights of Women*. London, 1792.

*Dictionary of National Biography*
*Report on the Differentiation of Curricula between the Sexes*. London, 1919.
(Board of Education Publication.)